KEEP THE BOOK OPEN

Beyond the Basics of Disaster Spiritual Care

Thomas E. Kadel

eLectio Publishing
Little Elm, TX
www.eLectioPublishing.com

Keep the Book Open: Beyond the Basics of Disaster Spiritual Care
By Thomas E. Kadel

Copyright 2017 by Thomas E. Kadel. All rights reserved.
Cover Design by eLectio Publishing.

ISBN-13: 978-1-63213-388-5

Published by eLectio Publishing, LLC
Little Elm, Texas
http://www.eLectioPublishing.com

Printed in the United States of America

5 4 3 2 1 eLP 21 20 19 18 17

The eLectio Publishing creative team is comprised of: Kaitlyn Campbell, Emily Certain, Lori Draft, Court Dudek, Jim Eccles, Sheldon James, and Christine LePorte.

Publisher's Note

The publisher does not have any control over and does not assume any responsibility for author or third-party websites or their content.

Who is this book for?

Disaster Spiritual Care responders who have received training and credentials through recognized disaster response agencies and are looking for useful information, protocols, and procedures that go beyond the normal basic training models.

Faith-based leaders who want guidance for working with members of their faith community and the general community following a disaster.

Behavioral Health responders who often hear spiritual questions as they work with survivors.

Government officials, including federal, state, and local emergency managers, who seek clearer descriptions of what Disaster Spiritual Care is and how to make use of this powerful response when organizing a response plan.

Members of faith communities who want to provide effective assistance to friends and neighbors who may well be experiencing the worst season of their lives.

Those who want to better understand the spiritual needs of those who have experienced a disaster—natural or human-caused.

This book addresses the spiritual needs of persons from all faith traditions as well as those who have no religious affiliation.

Though it regularly addresses Disaster Spiritual Care, those who respond from other response modes may find the material here helpful to better understand the spiritual needs of disaster survivors and the tools of those who serve them.

Thank You

This book is the result of a lot of help and support from so many people. I am grateful to you all.

To my wife, Lois, goes my deepest gratitude. You have supported and encouraged me, especially when my own confidence waned. You have always done this for me.

To our kids and grandkids, you are the joy that I float on, and I do float on it.

To colleagues over the years, please know that you have been my teachers and helpers with all that I have done.

To the Louisville Institute, your Pastoral Study Grant enabled me to have the time and resources that made this writing possible

To all of you and to so many others,

Thank you

CONTENTS

Overview
When Things Don't Add Up

When called to respond as a Disaster Spiritual Care responder, I often feel like I am parachuting into a jungle with a machete in my hand. I am going to land in an unfamiliar place with no clear path and serving the vague mission of "doing something helpful."

If I could get a printout of what I am thinking, the list would certainly include:

- How do I begin?
- Who should I talk with?
- What should I say?
- Am I up for this?
- How can I possibly help?
- Can I remember the things I've been trained to do?

From everything I've heard over the years, my thoughts probably resemble most other responders' thoughts. A leader in setting standards and procedures for Disaster Spiritual Care, the National Voluntary Organizations Active in Disaster (NVOAD) offers this explanation of what this care is. "Spiritual Care includes anything that assists an individual, family or community in drawing upon their own spiritual perspective as a source of strength, hope and healing. In disaster, anything that nurtures the human spirit in coping with the crisis is Spiritual Care" (National Voluntary Organizations Active in Disaster, "Light Our Way", 2013, p. 7).

There's the jungle—it is vast, undefined, and filled with things that are not a part of my everyday experience. If I were to compare this experience with my more regular life, I'd characterize my day-to-day life as visiting a national park. In the park, there are still unfamiliar things, but there are well-worn paths, signs pointing the way to things I might need, and, best of all, maps. I may be in the wilderness, but there are trusted pointers.

No amount of training will dispel the unfamiliar nature of a disaster response. I know I am quite likely to encounter people who

1

have just come through the worst experience of their lives. I know it's certai that trauma (the overwhelming of one's coping abilities) will be everywhere. I know that survivors will be coping the very best that they can. But I also know that their normal cognitive functioning will be impaired. Fear and terror may dominate. Confusion and anger may surround them like the very air they are breathing. This is a time of chaos for them. It is a time when nothing adds up. Most have never been through a disaster before, and this experience jumbles and overwhelms everything that they've come to expect from life. Everything in them will strain to carve some order out of this chaos.

Chaos leads to suffering, and suffering becomes a spiritual crisis.

NVOAD identifies a number of "spiritual dis-ease" symptoms that people may exhibit during and after a disaster:

- Reconsidering core tenets of religious beliefs
- Asking questions like "Why did God do this?"
- Questioning justice and meaning
- Feeling far from previously held beliefs
- Feeling a need to be cleansed
- Closing oneself off from loved ones
- Feeling despair and hopelessness
- Feeling guilty
- Wondering about life and death
- Feeling shame (National Voluntary Organizations Active in Disaster, "Light Our Way", 2013, p. 7)

Sometimes words will fail them and we will see them staring off into nowhere. They, too, have parachuted into this jungle. They, too, want—but will not find—safe, well-worn paths back to someplace familiar. They, too, have only a machete to clear a path for themselves.

But their machetes are not made of steel. Their machetes are the narrative understanding of their own lives. We will examine this machete, which all disaster survivors possess but may need assistance to find. And we'll see how, as Disaster Spiritual Care responders, we can help them re-discover these resources, if necessary, and help prepare them for the often-lengthy process of modifying their understanding of their lives in light of what they have been through. No person or community returns to "normal" after a disaster. Even the oft-used term "new normal" can be misleading, as it hints that life will be somewhat like life before the disaster. It is, for most, quite unlike that earlier life.

The World Turned Upside Down: Shattered Assumptions and Chaos

In the course of this book we will consider the nature of the disaster survivor's world and what they need when their world has been turned upside down. In 1781, General Lord Cornwallis surrendered at Yorktown. There were numerous accounts that, during surrender ceremony, the British band played the an old British song, "The World Turned Upside Down." The world had indeed been turned upside down. An untrained army of merchants and farmers had defeated the greatest military force on the face of the planet. It was stunning and unbelievable. Nothing fit into familiar understandings of how things of the world worked. Similarly, following a disaster, the world of survivors seems just as stunning and unbelievable.

The title of Ronnie Janoff-Bulman's 1992 book *Shattered Assumptions* is a powerful truth for most who experience a disaster. Her premise is that we each carry within us certain foundational assumptions about life and ourselves. She suggests that powerful life events can shatter those assumptions, leaving us with a non-functioning GPS system about life, its meaning, and our worthiness to live it. (Janoff-Bulman, 1992)

Using Janoff-Bulman's ideas as a starting point, we will explore how we experience those assumptions as a story-like dynamic within us. Much of that story is written below the level of our conscious awareness. When that story is shattered, we experience chaos, and chaos is nothing more and certainly nothing less than "things not

3

adding up" any more. It is when the world seems as if it has been turned upside down.

This is the point at which we meet many of those we will serve. We'll notice their valiant attempts to put things back into a story that does add up. None of us can tolerate chaos very long. Survivors will sometimes frantically search for additional information about the disaster or about its effects. They will endlessly seek cause and effect, action and consequence. This places many in the very vulnerable position of accepting anything that will give some order to the chaos. This may help provide them with some sense of order in the sea of chaos. But if that order is forged out of falsehood, there will likely be difficult consequences for them down the road.

Meaning in Narrative

Chaos is Ground Zero for Disaster Spiritual Care. This is where we will most often meet those who have experienced a disaster. They seem to be seeking answers. That is what their cognitive brain demands—something that adds up.

But they seek something else, too, something that is even more pressing and more necessary. They seek meaning. They will wonder what the experience means to the ones they love and the community they live in. How will things turn out? And beneath that is an even more important question: What does all of this mean for who *I* am? I know I'm different, but how? And what will it mean for me?

This is where something called Narrative Identity can be enormously useful. Narrative Identity describes the story-like way that we understand ourselves and the world we live in. True resiliency does not aim at exorcizing the disaster from one's story but focuses instead on discovering how this disaster experience modifies that story. Self-understanding takes the form of narrative. It is the story we live by.

Disaster Spiritual Care is well-suited to attending to this quest. But, as we'll see, our work can only help them begin this quest for a meaning-filled life story. The chances are slim that we'll be with them

4

for much more than the beginning of that quest. Thus, the title of this book is *Keep the Book Open*. If their lives can be thought of as a book, resiliency is built upon their anticipation that there is something more to come. We call this "hope." And there, finally, is a term that people of faith like spiritual care responders are familiar with.

Private and Public Response

This is perhaps a good point to pause and address an important distinction between "private" and "public" responses. A private response is one offered by members of a faith community to other members of that same faith community. In a private religious response, the customs, rituals, language, symbols, belief systems, and sacred texts are shared by the responder and those he or she will serve. This is a rich response in which all these shared things can be used to address suffering and keep the books of their lives open to hope. Hope can be framed from shared and familiar sacred texts. Meaning can emerge from shared rituals and symbols. Faith-based leaders are very prepared to use common understandings of divine presence to bring comfort and hope. These leaders do this all the time in their work with the dying, the grieving, the confused, and the seekers.

Public response, on the other hand, assumes that the spiritual care provider does not know or does not share a common faith context with those to be served. This is when a response is made to a larger or more diverse group of people. The spiritual care provider will most often be with people she or he has never met. And even if the one served has deep religious faith, the provider is not normally in a position to interpret that person's religious symbols and texts to them. That is why all good Disaster Spiritual Care training emphasizes connecting people with their own religious community where that rich private work can take place.

Both private and public response are vital. Yet they are different. One is not more important than the other. *Keep the Book Open* is primarily about public response, though some of the ideas here may be well used in a private response as well. Public response resources can be used in private response, but private response resources cannot be used in public response.

Hope Is the Core

With that in mind, remember that hope is at the core of all spirituality. Whether that hope anticipates life after death is a matter for religion and private response. Public Disaster Spiritual Care focuses on God's desire that beloved creations also experience rich and full life *before* death. Will there be a life following this disaster that is full and rich? In no way is this meant to place religious hope on a lower and less important plane. Quite the contrary. For those whose religious faith includes the anticipation of life after death, hope is extraordinarily important. This is especially true if the survivor has lost loved ones or had a near-death experience themselves.

But, in the context of Disaster Spiritual Care, spiritual hope is a different thing. It is also an extraordinarily important thing. It is at the core of questions like:

- "Am I worthy of life before death?"
- "Can life have meaning?"
- "Will the world permit me and those I love to experience a fulfilling and rich life before death?"
- "Can I feel alive again?"
- "How might life from now on be different than life before the disaster?"

This, again, is Ground Zero for our work.

Most Disaster Spiritual Care responders meet survivors relatively soon after a disaster. We may meet them as they are sorting through the rubble of their home that was destroyed by a tornado, in a shelter as they await flood waters to recede, or at a family assistance center while authorities sift through the aftereffects of a human-caused disaster. We may meet them within a few hours of the disaster or perhaps a week or two later. But in most cases, we will meet them only a few times and most often only once. We are not likely to be with them for the entirety of their quest for meaning.

Though our time with them is likely to be short, if we are able to assist them to keep the book of their lives open to hope, our impact will remain with them the remainder of their lives.

Trauma and Re-Trauma

Understanding trauma is a necessity in spiritual care. When people experience trauma, they are not in their right minds. That is not an insult; it is a statement of scientific fact. The brain literally functions differently under stress. Knowing something about the brain and how the limbic system works helps us recognize trauma's effects on those we serve. This will help us explain why a common style of caring for someone that works well in ordinary circumstances may actually damage someone in the grip of trauma.

If a young girl, for instance, had a bad day at school, her mom will sit with her at the end of that day and say, "Tell me what happened." Then would come questions about how she feels about what happened. As the young girl tells the story, she "gets it out" of herself. She unburdens her heart of the memories and feelings that made the day bad. It can seem like a cleansing experience. As the young girl tells her story and Mom listens, something important between parent and child happens. Feelings can be affirmed, support offered, and encouragement given as the two talk. This is how a bad day gets sorted out.

But one who has been traumatized by a disaster may experience the "getting it out" altogether differently. Because trauma overwhelms one's ability to cope, the act of re-telling the story of the disaster may actually re-traumatize that person. Past, present, and future get all muddled together in the traumatized person's brain. When that young girl tells about her bad day, she is describing something that happened in the past. When a traumatized person describes the events of a disaster, he or she may well re-experience it as if it were happening again in the present moment. For the traumatized person, time loses much of its distinction between past, present, and future. This order, which in other circumstances seems so common and natural, often congeals into an inseparable mass.

While this certainly doesn't happen for everyone, we will have a couple ways of knowing ahead of time by observation who it may happen to. There are indicators that some may show, however. For instance, one whose emotional affect is numb may be seeking a defense against the pain of their emotions. Likewise, one who is displaying very high emotional affect may be right then in the grip of the disaster.

On the other hand, some people will show a strong need to tell their story; when they express that need, we will listen with care and acceptance. But it is important to avoid prying. Follow them to whatever level they lead us, but do not attempt to encourage them to go beyond that. They will let us know if they need to tell the story of their experience of the disaster. But until they do, we avoid asking them to tell the story or even hinting that we would like them to tell.

Listening with Story Ears

By using a Narrative Identity approach, we can avoid prying into their experience of the disaster and instead embrace with them the very inner resources and life meanings they have used to get this far. They will use these life meanings as they head into what will surely seem an uncertain future.

To do this we draw from the field of Narrative Identity. It helps us know how to listen to their *lives* rather than just to the story of the disaster. Our ears become story sensitive ears and will be tuned to hear themes called agency and community. We listen for whether that person seems to expect things to get better (redemption) or worse (contamination). And through all of that, we remain aware of the importance of identifying the story as "thick" or "thin" and what that may tell us.

Resiliency is a key word for all disaster modes, not just spiritual care. We stay aware that many people seem to have a "built-in" set of resources that helps them rebound from a disaster – whether they receive care or not. Estimates suggest that about half of the population fits this description.

An Eye Toward Others

We will serve side-by side with other responders. Our work includes serving them, too. Secondary trauma is real and can be just as debilitating as the first-hand trauma experienced by those who were in the middle of the disaster. These responders may also need our care.

Likewise, self-care is not optional. But how do we deal with things that have overwhelmed our own coping abilities?

This book will conclude with some "what if" questions related to the possibility of broad secondary trauma that may be affecting large parts of the American population. I will urge all of us to share our own ideas about this and whether this might become a new frontier for Disaster Spiritual Care.

Finally, *Keep the Book Open* is not intended as a full Disaster Spiritual Care training course. It builds upon common basic training learnings. Therefore, there will be references—but not full coverages—of ideas and practices usually treated in the basic courses. Please consider this a tool—one of many tools we have to use.

Chaplain Naomi Paget was on scene in northern Colorado, an area which had just been devastated by a wild land fire. While there, she spoke with an elderly man who had lost his home to the terrible fire. All he had left was a scrapbook. He was distraught and had no idea if he could carry on. The two sat together and went through the precious memories contained in that book. He would tell stories about the pictures and sadly recall the life he once had. When he came to the last page in the album it was blank.

"I wonder what you will put on that page," said Chaplain Paget.

1

When Souls Are Exposed

Can There Be Life Again Before Death?

"When you come to the edge of all the light you know, and are about to step off into the darkness of the unknown, faith is knowing one of two things will happen: There will be something solid to stand on, or you will be taught how to fly."

-Patrick Overton

Disaster Spiritual Care can largely be summed up in Chaplain Paget's comment, "I wonder what you will put on that page." Care with and for those who have lost so much to a natural or human-caused disaster is about helping them keep the books of their lives open to hope. That yet-to-be-filled page represents the future. And though they may have no idea what will go onto that page, the very truth that there *is* a page is a powerful symbol for hope. What an entirely different experience it would have been for this man had Chaplain Paget simply closed the book and thanked him for showing it to her!

Hope is the fuel for recovery and the energy of resiliency. We may want to write that on the inside of our foreheads so we can look there and be reminded of the core of Disaster Spiritual Care.

Disaster Spiritual Care is among the youngest of the disaster response modes. It is only now growing into maturity and still has much growing to do. It is focused on assisting survivors keep the books of their lives open to the surprising grace of God. It is about helping them embrace the reality that there can once again be life before death.

Even with those who have no religious inclination, the human spirit longs for meaning, hope, and purpose—the "stuff" of

11

spirituality. Without even mentioning God, Chaplain Paget introduced spirituality into their conversation. She used that blank page as a pointer to the future and to her own belief in the extraordinary and usually quiet ways that God works in human lives. This seems particularly true in the wake of suffering.

Narrative Identity psychologist Dan McAdams reminds us that, in *The Varieties of Religious Experience*, the great philosopher William James observed that "all the world's great religions begin with the problem of human suffering." McAdams goes on:

> Suffering originates in human flaws or frailties of some sort, or in the very nature of human existence. Thus, Christians and Jews speak of original sin whereas Buddhists ascribe suffering to dukkha, which denotes universal human conflict and sorrow. Each religious tradition suggests what human beings need to do or experience in order to be delivered from suffering to a positive state (McAdams, Jones, & Altmaier (Ed.), 2016).

Chaplain Paget's purpose was not to convert the grieving man to any particular religious expression but to open his heart to life after disaster. To do that, she simply yet powerfully connected his future to his past—integrated the potential meaning of his future life into the already experienced meaning of his life to this point.

Enfleshed Presence

One of the prime goals of Disaster Spiritual Care is to help keep the book open for those who have experienced a disaster. Perhaps they have lost everything. They may not even be able to imagine the future. Yet Disaster Spiritual Care responders hold to the conviction that each of us has both the resources and the grit to step into an unknown future. That is what we call resiliency.

It is important to know how to listen to survivors' stories without risking re-traumatizing them. It is never good to pry disaster stories out of survivors. Instead, responders enflesh the presence of the divine in the way they listen. Through that enfleshed presence, we become a channel of healing damaged hope.

Using an approach based upon Narrative Identity, this process listens for the stories that people tell about themselves rather than their stories about the disaster experience itself. All of us have been, are, and will always be people of our own stories. When one's story has been shattered sufficiently and that hope for the future doesn't add up, this process holds the promise to keep the book open so that hope can emerge from their own inner resources. Enfleshed presence is a very powerful thing. It describes a unique way of being with someone in which we become the physical presence of God, expressed in the careful and sensitive listening to the lives of others as if they were the sacred things that they actually are.

So why do we call this "spiritual" care?

Spiritual issues can bubble up from just about anywhere when one has experienced a disaster. On June 12, 2016, forty-nine persons were killed in an Orlando nightclub, and fifty-three were wounded. The nation watched in horror that day as the chaos slowly gave way to the awful reality of what happened. One wounded survivor, twenty-year-old Patience Carter of Philadelphia, lost her best friend, Akyra. From her hospital a couple days later, Patience told the story of that terrible night. Her deep distress was apparent. She had escaped the nightclub to apparent safety but then realized her friend wasn't with her. She went back in and found her friend, and they hid in a bathroom. Then the gunman came in. Patience was shot in both legs. She shared the gory details of looking around and seeing the wounded and the dead. Then she saw the lifeless body of her friend.

On June 14, before she described those awful events for the press, she said she wanted to share a poem she had written.

> *The guilt of feeling grateful to be alive is heavy.*
>
> *Wanting to smile about surviving but not sure if the people around you are ready.*

As the world mourns the victims killed and viciously slain,
I feel guilty about screaming about my legs in pain.

Because I could feel nothing like the other 49 who weren't
so lucky to feel this pain of mine.

I never thought in a million years that this could happen.

I never thought in a million years that my eyes could
witness something so tragic.

Looking at the souls leaving the bodies of individuals,
looking at the killer's machine gun throughout my right
peripheral.

Looking at the blood and debris covered on everyone's faces.
Looking at the gunman's feet under the stall as he paces.

The guilt of feeling lucky to be alive is heavy.

It's like the weight of the ocean's walls crushing
uncontrolled by levies.

It's like being drug through the grass with a shattered leg
and thrown on the back of a Chevy.

It's like being rushed to the hospital and told you're gonna
make it when you laid beside individuals whose lives were
brutally taken.

The guilt of being alive is heavy (Ferguson, 2016).

Many have experienced this deep and awful kind of "survivor guilt." It pulses in a hot flow. It is the soul stretching heavenward and crying, "Why me? Why them?"

There is likely a no more spiritual cry than this. And it doesn't matter whether that cry comes from someone who has had a rich religious life or from one who believes that there is no God; it is the same cry. Whether someone has religion or not, each person has this spiritual core. Disaster Spiritual Care attends to that spiritual core. It is a high calling and a sacred privilege to have someone expose their soul and its wounds to us.

14

It is an exposure that seeks to make sense out of no-sense, meaning out of no-meaning, and life purpose out of unfocused chaos.

Summary

Each person has a spiritual core—a yearning for something or someone bigger and more powerful than themselves that can relieve suffering, provide protection, and restore meaning.. This yearning surfaces powerfully in the wake of suffering. The mission of Disaster Spiritual Care is to help survivors discover a pathway into themselves where they can re-discover their own resources for hope. But responders avoid prying out stories of their disaster experience that they are not ready to share. These life experience resources are accessible in a narrative form and emerge as people tell about themselves. We become the enfleshed presence of God as we listen to their lives, not their disaster stories. Their lives are much more than this disaster. This enfleshed presence opens the door to hope and the possibility that one can once again experience life before death.

Preview

Enfleshing the presence of God in the way we listen to the stories of people's lives is a powerful thing. But how do we do it?

Living life bears a resemblance to writing a story. At the end of each sentence there is a period. Whatever follows that period is unlimited. The story can proceed in any direction. But it will not proceed in any direction until the writer makes a decision about what comes next. This is true for life and the living of it. Yet that decision is strongly influenced by the assumptions about life that we carry within us. Narrative Identity strategies assist responders with hearing those assumptions and how they influence the story of life we write moment to moment.

2
Let Me Tell You My Story

How Do Stories Work?

"He wanted to know where stories came from.

Cohn said from other stories.

"Where did they come from?"

Somebody spoke a metaphor and that broke into a story. Man began to tell them to keep his life from washing away.

"Which was the first story?"

"God inventing Himself."

"How did He do thot?" [sic]

"He began, He's the God of Beginnings. He said the word and the earth began. If you tell stories you can say what God's doing. Let's read that one again, Buz." He turned to the story of creation (Malamud, 1982, p. 70).

When we say that it is vital to be with survivors as the enfleshed presence of God, we are speaking of more than the simple act of being with another. Physical presence is vital, but it is only part of what we are calling enfleshed presence. Enfleshed presence requires us to bring all of ourselves to all of the person we are serving. We bring the story we understand ourselves to be to the story the survivor understands him or herself to be. Story is present with story. But how does this work?

It is accurate, but simplistic, to define a story as plot, character, and location. Even a very brief short story is the result of thousands upon thousands of choices. Each time the author places a period at the end of a sentence, a complicated process begins. The period signals the end of a thought. But it is also a crisis point. The story goes nowhere until the author makes a choice about where the story goes next. And the possibilities are literally endless. The story stays stuck until the author makes a choice. The author writes that next sentence, and the cycle begins all over again.

Montraldo

One of the classic story first sentences appeared in the June 6, 1964 issue of *The New Yorker*. John Cheever's story "Montraldo" began with this classic sentence: "The first time I robbed Tiffany's, it was raining" (Cheever, "Montraldo", 1964).

Where is this story going? What would be the next sentence? Is this story about a robber's life or about rain? Did the robber actually rob Tiffany's, or is that person simply a grandiose liar? Is the story about how many times this person robbed Tiffany's, or it is about what the person actually took? Could it be leading in a direction that has nothing to do with the first line? One might even wonder if John Cheever himself knew where the story was going. The story could be going anywhere. It turns out to be a tale that will feature an old lady and her maid in an Italian villa that has no toilets, adultery, a priest acting unpriestly, and too many other twists and turns to count.

Imagine being handed a piece of paper that was blank except for Cheever's first line and told to finish the story. That story would likely bear no resemblance to "Montraldo." The difference between what I would write and what Cheever did write is that his imagination is far less inhibited than my own, and his life experience and my own are built of two different sets of events and assumptions.

Something that may reduce the number of choices for me would be if I were given these additional instructions: "Your story must be about things getting worse for the central character." Now the range of possibilities for the next sentence may be reduced somewhat. "Your story must also feature the main character struggling to discover a way to be effective at something" would further restrict the next sentence possibilities. But the possibilities haven't been limited all that much. They are still not countable. However, the story would not proceed at all until I made a choice.

Understanding Ourselves Narratively

Living life is very much like writing a story. In fact, many studies show that we understand lives narratively. Each moment presents us with a period at the end of a sentence. What happens next is filled with nearly endless possibilities. But our stories cannot proceed until we have chosen what we will fill that next moment with. For instance, imagine that someone places a piece of key lime pie before me. Will I eat it, or will I pass it up? Whichever of those two choices I make will affect me—even if in a very small way— and the rest of my life. Are you familiar with the Butterfly Effect from Chaos Theory? It suggests that the flapping of a butterfly's beautiful wings will affect weather all around the planet. Then, of course, eating or not eating that piece of pie are not my only choices, are they? They are only the most obvious ones. I could choose any number of different things. I could smoosh it into someone's face, make a speech about hunger in the world, offer it to someone else. There may be choices that seem obvious to us, but there are also always a lot of other not-so-obvious ones as well.

We do not make those choices in a vacuum. What if I believe that I am destined to be fat? Would that affect my choice? What if I once saw someone choke on a bite of key lime pie? What if I am angry or happy? Any one of these things could affect the choice I make next.

But beneath the surface of even seemingly unimportant choices (think of them as next sentences in my life), like what to do with that piece of key lime pie, there is a whole world of influences of which I may or may not be aware of. And it is quite likely that the more important I perceive a choice to be, the stronger its below-the-surface influence will be.

Cognitive psychologists won't ever run out of work as they seek to understand our choices, why we make the ones we make, and what influences played key roles in our decisions.

This may all be interesting for us to ponder, but it goes to a different level when we think of someone whose whole life has been changed by disaster. The disaster has placed a period at the end of a sentence. Where will this person's story go from here? This is where enfleshed presence becomes powerful.

Those below-the-surface influences—some conscious to us and some unconscious—have been called by a variety of names. The conscious ones have been called "Mundane Story" and "Narrative Identity." Unconscious ones have been called "Sacred Story", "Personal Myth", "Assumptive World", and "Schema." There is nothing magical about these various labels, though researchers may define them somewhat differently. What is important is that our story-like inner narratives are highly influential in tipping the scale toward one choice or another whether we are aware of it or not.

Three Fundamental Assumptions

Janoff-Bulman proposes that there are three fundamental assumptions that live within each of us and that they are enormously powerful in their structuring of our expectations and hence our choices. Her three archetypal assumptions are:

- The world is benevolent.
- The world is meaningful.
- The self is worthy (Janoff-Bulman, 1992, p. 6).

These assumptions inform and help shape the stories we live. The expectation of benevolence gives rise to trust. Meaningfulness fuels hope and purpose. Worthiness is the yeast of self-respect and the presumption that we will be treated respectfully.

Of course, we know that all people do not share equal quantities of these assumptions. Think of them as scales:

Cruel	**World is**	*Benevolent*

Meaningless	**World is**	*Meaningful*

Worthless	**Self is**	*Worthy*

Wherever we may find ourselves on those scales has plenty to do with the Assumptive Story we carry with us. The Assumptive Story has, in turn, plenty to do with the choices we make or, if you will, the next sentences in our Narrative Identity story.

One additional important factor identified by Janoff-Bulman is that a person's inner assumptions or schema is very resistant to change and tends to reject ideas, motives, and even hopes that conflict with it. The data of our lives is unlikely to alter the schema under normal circumstances. New and conflicting life data tends to become separated from the core schema, and we are likely to treat it as a separate thing altogether. Here is how that works.

An Alternate Schema

Let's say there are Green People and Blue People in the world. A Green Person named Pat has a generalized schema that Blue People are inept and somehow inferior to him and other Green People. But along comes a Blue Person named Fred who is quite competent in many things. One would hope that Fred would weaken or dismantle Pat's schema. But since schemas are so change resistant, Pat is likely to do something else. He begins to stop seeing Fred as a Blue Person and instead constructs an alternate schema about people named Fred. Fred the person becomes a prototype of Fred the schema. Fred, as a competent Blue person, is discounted. The schema about Blue People is little affected. By the way, if this sounds like a real life analysis of race relations, so be it.

The point here is that the stuff in our schemas about life do not easily change even when confronted with conflicting life data.

"Research," Janoff-Bulman says, "suggests that schemas persist even in the face of contradictory evidence. Often this is the case because we are able simply to discount the new information" (Janoff-Bulman, 1992, p. 34). Let's refer to this new and discounted construction as an alternative schema.

So, we've identified several aspects of being a living story. Here's a summary:

- Each moment in life provides a period to the previous "sentence" in our lives.
- The choices for the next "sentence" are practically unlimited.
- The story can't move on until a decision is made about that next "sentence."
- While the possibilities are practically endless, they are strongly influenced by both conscious and unconscious narratives we hold within us.
- The strength or weakness of our belief in three basic assumptions about life and our living of it are the yeast of both our conscious and unconscious self-narratives—our schema.
- Our schema is very resistant to change and modification and rejects data that conflicts with it.
- Alternative schemas may be created from the rejected basic schemas.

Where is this leading, and what does it have to do with caring for those whose lives have been affected by the trauma of a disaster? Each of these aspects of Narrative Identity may have key roles to play in the care we design and deliver—our enfleshed presence.

Summary

Being the enfleshed presence of God with another requires that we bring the whole of ourselves to the whole of the other. A vital part of that process is allowing our life story to touch the life story of another.

Living life bears a remarkable similarity to writing a story. In both instances the choice for whatever comes next is nearly unlimited. But whatever comes next in real life is strongly influenced by both conscious and unconscious assumptions and stories that we have accumulated over the course of life. In fact, we understand ourselves through these narratives. And the narratives themselves contain themes or schemas. These schemas become firmly rooted in us and are not easily changed. We are more likely to develop an alternative schema to contain new life information that contradicts the key schemas.

Preview

Let's meet a part of the brain that has helped human beings live long enough to become human beings—the amygdala. It is a very old part of the limbic system and plays an enormously important role in how we react to threats—in fact, even in assessing whether something is a threat at all. The amygdala's work is a key factor in how people experience a disaster. It is where trauma begins. Without understanding the amygdala, our work with survivors may be far less effective than it could be.

3

With Friends Like Amygdala . . .

How Your Brain Processes Trauma

"He says he can't stop the vision of the flames in the next door house and hears again and again the screams of those residents..."

Imagine for a moment that you are taking an idyllic walk through a heavily wooded forest. The sun is shining brightly, and the walk feels wonderful. You've noticed wild flowers and birds, and some of the views have been breathtaking. As you are walking along, though, you suddenly see a bear! What do you do?

Wait—don't answer too quickly!

Your response would almost certainly depend upon where that bear is, wouldn't it?

If the bear is a few hundred yards away on another hill, you just might feel excitement, reach for your binoculars and watch that bear as long as you could. This sighting just adds to the wonder of an already very special day. You can't wait to tell people! Your heart races with excitement, and you stand as still and as quietly as you possibly can and watch this rare and wonderful sight.

If, on the other hand, that bear appears unexpectedly from behind a tree a just few yards from you, everything will be different, won't it? Something we commonly call the "fight, flight, or freeze" response kicks in. You will likely jump back and take instant action. You may flee. You may fight, though that might not be wise in this case. You may freeze, possum-like—less wise, still. Whatever you do, you will need strength, focus, protection from possible wounds, and a number of other assets, including dissociation.

Let's say you begin to run. You didn't take time to reason this through, but your legs are moving! Your response was automatic. You may notice that you are running faster than usual and feeling

25

stronger than usual. You may not notice that even your body's blood flow has changed, sending more blood to protect your vital organs and brain and less to your extremities—which is handy if you run through thorns and is especially handy if the bear should catch up to you! Also, you may not notice it as you run, but your range of perceptual awareness has narrowed significantly. You are not taking in the beauty of your surroundings any more. That would slow you down and distract you from your main task—survival. You are focused completely on the escape path.

The same thing—sighting a bear—can cause dramatically different responses depending on whether something in you perceives the bear as a threat. And you can thank your amygdala. Your amygdala is actually two small parts of your brain right behind your forehead and is part of your limbic system—the very primitive part of the brain that has helped you and other human beings live long enough to actually become human beings.

Your amygdala is paired up with your neo-cortex. The neo-cortex is a newer part of your brain and triggers cognitive (thinking/reasoning) processes in you.

An over-simplified version of what happened there in the forest is that you saw the bear and another part of your brain, the thalamus, relayed that sighting to both the amygdala and the neo-cortex. The signal went about twice as fast to the amygdala, though, because it has the responsibility to give you the very quickest assessment of the risk that the bear poses. Before your thinking mind was aware that you had even seen the bear your amygdala had already made that assessment and begun your response.

This is related to an experience you have likely had many times. You are driving in your car and something—a ball or an animal or a child—jumps out in front of the car. You slam on the brakes and avoid the problem. You didn't think about slamming on the brakes; you realized that you *had* slammed on the brakes. When the thalamus sends the perception of something to both the amygdala and the neo-cortex, the amygdala will assess the risk and initiate action before the neo-cortex even receives the information!

If the bear in that earlier example is no threat, the amygdala signals the neo-cortex that it is okay to figure out how to enjoy the bear sighting.

But if that "reptilian" part of your brain assesses the bear to be a threat, something entirely different begins to happen within you. That perceived threat (the nearby bear, the stressor) will turn on a complex set of changes in you. A whole range of things will take place. And all of it will seek to assist you with surviving the sudden appearance of the nearby bear.

Why a Bear?

Now, here are some things to think about. We've all seen bears on TV and know from other sources that bears can threaten much weaker human beings. We take that for granted. But in that first instant, you haven't gone to your mental filing cabinet and looked up "meeting a bear in the forest." Something in the amygdala told you a threat was present – probably something stored there from primitive human experience with bears. The amygdala gave you an instant reaction, one that you didn't have to process cognitively. The twelve millisecond difference in reactions between the amygdala and the neo-cortex doesn't sound like much, but it could be the difference between life and death.

By sending the "fear" signal, the amygdala warned you to fight or flee—or maybe even freeze—rather than try to pet it as you might have if it had been a little puppy. Once the signal was sent to you, your reaction triggered all those physical and neurological changes.

But most of us do not live in the forest anymore. Rarely, if ever in a lifetime, will a bear pop out from behind a tree at close range. Other threats will appear. The amygdala may initiate an action that does not match the circumstances of our modern life.

If the Amygdala Only Knew

So, what if that same series of stimuli and responses is triggered by something we cannot fight or flee from? What if the life-threatening stimulus does not provide a resolution to the threat? That is, what if we can't escape it or protect a loved one from it? The amygdala served primitive humans quite well, but the world has changed significantly since then and we don't encounter bears very often. But many people do encounter threats from disaster—whether natural or human-caused.

The amygdala can be a life-saving friend, or it can set the stage for the experience of trauma. The American Psychological Association describes trauma as

> ...an emotional response to a terrible event like an accident, rape or natural disaster. Immediately after the event, shock and denial are typical. Longer term reactions include unpredictable emotions, flashbacks, strained relationships and even physical symptoms like headaches or nausea. While these feelings are normal, some people have difficulty moving on with their lives. Psychologists can help these individuals find constructive ways of managing their emotions (American Psychological Association, "Trauma", 2016).

We could easily add combat, terrorism, and other present day threats to their list. What is clear is that the amygdala does not have "be rational" in its job description.

Suddenly that amygdala turns on us. It is impossible to fight a tornado or hurricane or flood. The suddenness of a terrorist bomb provides no opportunity to flee or fight. But those are the responses that the amygdala knows how to initiate. However, fleeing or fighting may not handle the threat. The amygdala has registered something it is unfamiliar with but relies on the familiar (and useless) ways of trying to escape the threat.

Two separate but related things happen when disaster strikes. There is the hard-wired reaction of the amygdala (the running, fighting or freezing, the perceptual changes, the blood flow) awaiting a resolution. As far as the amygdala is concerned, the threat hasn't been handled, and it steadfastly continues to do its job of trying to save us.

In our modern age, there is another factor that the amygdala just isn't prepared to understand. That is a secondhand experience that is called "secondary trauma." Those of us old enough to remember can likely recall having been riveted to a TV or radio on September 11, 2001. Even if we were nowhere near New York, Washington, D.C., or Shanksville, we likely felt threatened. Our perceptual range narrowed to the continuing coverage of the attacks. No longer were we aware of the beautiful day, the taste of the food we consumed, or the day's anticipated routine. Everything changed. We were experiencing a secondhand threat and possibly secondhand trauma. Noticed or unnoticed, the amygdala's perceptions initiated a response designed to protect. The disconnect is that we do not need protection from something viewed on television. Remember, "be rational" is not in the amygdala's job description. Think of a news story about a faraway hurricane. It, too, can initiate an irrational flight or fight response. We react with all the appropriate reactions but to an inappropriate threat. Severe cases of trauma may result in Post-Traumatic Stress Disorder when those triggers and our responses to them are out of our control and we find ourselves in an altogether different place and time, perhaps facing a quite different and overwhelming threat.

He's All Right, But...

A young man sits in a reception center set up for persons affected by a tragic house fire. Three people had perished in a rowhome fire in an urban center. The young man stares into space. His house, directly next door, had been damaged by smoke and water, but he and the others in that house were not injured.

A Disaster Spiritual Care responder (DSC) is alerted to his distress by a caseworker. "He says he can't stop the vision of the flames in the next door house and hears again and again the screams of those residents." The young man speaks only Spanish, so the DSC responder asks an interpreter to help him communicate with him. He tells of the fire in a monotone and emotionless voice. His face is blank, and his mind seems somewhere else. The interpreter faithfully assists the conversation. Suddenly, the DSC sees the interpreter's eyes go wide and she gasps. After a moment, the interpreter looks at the DSC and says, "One of the people screaming from the windows was his best friend." A long pause. "And that friend was one of the three who perished." Suddenly things come into clear focus for the DSC. The young man saw and heard his friend pleading for help and could do nothing.

The replaying of the scene was likely due to those amygdala-triggered responses. His inner system kept replaying the scene, hoping to discover a way to save his friend's life. He was still—hours later—looking for something to do to make things turn out right. To fight the overwhelm, he shuts down and emotionally goes away.

The DSC shows compassion and responds to the man's request for a prayer for his friend, but the DSC quickly turns the conversation away from having the young man describe the fire any further. At this early moment, such a probing would not help and may very well result in adding to his trauma. When the conversation was over, the DSC tells the caseworker that follow-up is strongly recommended, provided by a behavioral or mental health worker experienced in treating trauma.

In this young man's case, the threat to his own life had been minimal, but painful trauma had resulted from the impossibility of saving his friend. His amygdala was still sending fight or flee signals, but they would have no impact on the loss of his friend. Instead, he fled to a numbed place within himself where he could temporarily not feel anything. Without effective treatment, the possibility exists for him to continue to relive the trauma of that day. It could come from a TV report of another fire, from a shout he hears, from the smell of smoke from a nearby barbeque grill, or from just about anything else that he had perceived (knowingly or unknowingly) during that fire. "Meaningless stimuli that occur in connection with trauma…can later trigger fear and stress themselves. Evolutionarily speaking, these kinds of associations help us anticipate harm. But sometimes, they also end up tying us up in knots" (Gonsales, *Surviving Survival: The Art and Science of Resilience*, 2012, p. 26).

Many, including those who treat war veterans suffering from PTSD, believe that trauma and PTSD are injuries rather than emotional events. Though the 2013 release of the Diagnostic and Statistical Manual of Mental Disorders (DSM-V) didn't classify PTSD as an anxiety disorder but rather as a category unto itself, many voices maintained that it should have been identified as an injury. Whatever trauma and PTSD are, they are significant and life-changing. Psychologist Froma Walsh notes

> When traumatic loss is suffered, we should not expect resolution in the sense of some complete, 'once-and-for-all' getting over it. Thus, resilience should not be seen as readily getting 'closure' on the experience or simply bouncing back and moving on. Recovery is a gradual process over time. Various facets of grief may alternate and reemerge with unexpected intensity, particularly with anniversaries and other nodal events (Walsh, "Traumatic Loss and Major Disasters: Strengthening Family and Community Resilience", 2007, p. 208).

Stay in Your Lane

One of the best practices for DSCs is, as one responder puts it, to "stay in your lane." This has implications for all who work with trauma sufferers. Disaster Spiritual Care responders, no matter what other training they have had, should not suddenly change lanes and become mental health responders. For that matter, mental health responders should not open up avenues to deliver deeper treatment when opportunities to pursue it may not be possible.

There is a special concern for clergy DSC responders that is embedded in the wisdom of staying in your lane. In the day-to-day practice of ministry, clergy are called upon to do many diverse things. They can find themselves in many different lanes. One of those lanes is pastoral counseling—an often generalized term that can refer to anything from giving advice to long term in-depth counseling. Sometimes it refers to a style of counseling specific to the faith tradition of that particular clergyperson and uses beliefs and symbols of that faith expression.

Perhaps more than most other professions that seek to help others, a clergyperson's responsibilities touch many other disciplines including therapy, counseling, case management, and so on. It is very important for these well-trained professionals to also know their boundaries. If one is clergy and also serving as a DSC, stay in that important DSC lane. Resist the urge to slide over into behavioral and/or mental health areas that are beyond normal clergy training. So, staying in your lane has two meanings for clergy. First, we don't switch roles. Second, we stay within our training and make referrals to the mental health professionals when appropriate.

In addition, in the immediate hours, days, and even months following a disaster, a tremendous amount of information about the disaster may yet be unknown. Affected persons may ask, "Why?" The cry may be for information about the cause of the disaster—as in the case of human-caused terrorist attacks or an airline disaster. DSCs also know that the "Why?" cry may be sent to the heavens, seeking a greater power's response out of anguish. This is a spiritual cry even for those who profess no "religious" beliefs. In either case, the cry comes from a part of us that cannot tolerate the chaos of not knowing.

Thick and Thin Answers

It is at this point that the sufferer is very vulnerable to "thin" answers. A thin answer is one that seeks to give false or incomplete answers. They are simplistic. Thick answers, on the other hand, contain much more detail, context, complexity, and emotional content. While thin answers may be comforting in the immediate term and possibly even mitigate the amygdala's alarm, they can pose great difficulty in the long term. To one who has experienced a traumatic event, a thin answer—no matter how well-intentioned—may well set that person up for another loss when its thinness is discovered. We should never seek to answer a "Why?" question unless we know for certain that our answer is accurate, and that is rarely possible, especially for early responders. It is always best practice not to even attempt such answers since even today's "certain truth" may be discarded tomorrow if new information comes to light.

Thin answers are a responder's ineffective attempts to deal with the trauma quickly and will often show as such. Even if it is unlikely that a firmer truth will be uncovered (as in the case of a "Why?" cast heavenward), the thin answer may well cause harm to that person's personal narrative story. It can be life-changing, for instance, if we describe a hurricane as an "act of God." Hurricane Katrina was often called an Act of God. This is usually said as a kind of shorthand to describe something out of human control. But the shorthand can easily be heard as an answer. Staying in your lane also includes resisting the impulses to guess or invent a cause for the disaster, as well as being aware of any shorthand language we may be tempted to use.

As responders we are likely to hear much conjecture spoken as fact. It is often difficult to distinguish the one from the other. As important as information is to an affected person, the information must be accurate, or it may very well cause more trouble. Before sharing anything, double and triple check information that is available before sharing it. Even then, measure the consequences should that information—despite all our efforts—prove to be incomplete or false. Though these cautions may seem to have little to do with spiritual care, any of them may hold the potential to influence one's Narrative Identity, and this, in turn, has the potential to affect that person's well-being and sense of hope.

Thin and Thick Stories

I mentioned thick and thin answers. But there is also something we will call thick and thin *stories*. Let's look at this more deeply.

I would like to tell you about my dad, Ralph. He was a kind, gentle, and caring man.

Dad was an infantry soldier in World War II. Like so many men and women of what Tom Brokaw labelled "the Greatest Generation," he spoke very little about his wartime experiences. I do know that he was part of the Allied Invasion of Anzio in Italy in January 1944.

The invasion was successful, but, due to command-level confusion, the Allies were ordered to dig in on the beach rather than to press their advantage. Some have called this one of the biggest American blunders of the war. The Nazis responded and pinned them down there until May. Dad told of hearing literally thousands of artillery shells bombarding them for those many weeks, always telling his story with a kind of emotionless description. He spoke most often of the "Screaming Mimis"—the whistling of the incoming shells. There were 29,000 American casualties at Anzio by the time they broke through the German lines. The combat was often fierce. But Dad never spoke of his fright.

Later, the Third Division, of which he was a part, made it to Rome and then was sent to be a part of the invasion of Southern France at St. Tropez only six months after Anzio. He and the others then fought their way northward through small French villages for weeks. In one such abandoned village, he and his sergeant were searching a house when a patrol of Nazi soldiers drove in. The two of them, alone in the village, heard the vehicles and then orders barked in German. As they hid in the basement, they heard two soldiers enter the house and begin to search it. One soldier came halfway down the basement steps and looked around but did not spot the two Americans. When the German got back to the top of the steps, he paused and threw a grenade into the basement, and it rolled near them. They could hear the two soldiers quickly run from the house. Dad could see the grenade roll toward them and then stop. But it did not go off. They waited there in silence for a long time; after hearing the German vehicles drive off, they carefully slipped out of the house and quickly ran back to their unit.

I heard Dad tell of this event twice; both times he told it without emotion. It sounded more like a log entry than a story.

He told few other stories. One, however, was a humorous account of the time he was ordered to drive a tank to a different French town with no idea of how to operate the thing. He told this story in great detail and with much laughter. He told of driving it into a deep ditch and later running over an abandoned vehicle that he couldn't figure out how to steer around. Another story featured a brief time when he was ordered to serve as an MP and how he was suddenly hated by his friends who were drinking in a secured French town. Again, much detail and even more laughter. These were stories thick with detail and emotion.

Dad fought his way through France and ended up in Austria as the war ended. I know his route by reading about the Third Division's exploits. But he never filled in any details. The most frequently told story of his war experience featured the very end of his enlistment time—after Germany had surrendered—when, as he was processed out, he ordered an Army surplus jeep. He joked for decades about whether that day just might be the day it would arrive.

But there was one more story he told to me. He told it just once and prefaced it by saying he had never told this story to another person—not even Mom. I was an adult, and he was well into middle age. We were driving through town when he suddenly said, "Tom, I know this sounds crazy, but there was a time in France when we were under heavy attack. I was so scared. And here's the crazy part— I looked up at the sky, and I swear to you, I saw God." He became very quiet but then added, "I shouldn't have mentioned this." I saw tears running down his cheeks. He never mentioned it again. I have longed to have that moment back and to ask Dad if we could pray and thank God for appearing to him and bringing him home safely. I have long carried the burden of believing that I failed him that day. He had reached out to me with a sacred memory and I didn't know what to say. I just hope my silence signaled my embrace of him and of his story. This story was brief but thick with meaning and emotion.

That was it. These were the only stories he ever told.

Passionless and thin stories about near-death. Detailed and humorous thick stories about a few safer things. And one deeply felt one that may have been the richest of all but that he immediately closed the door on.

Mom told me that after he returned from Europe, he didn't sleep well. when he did sleep, he would awaken nightly in terror. This recurred again and again until his death at seventy-five. Startle responses were common for him for the remainder of his life. I remember an occasion when, as a teenager, I had misbehaved and was probably a smart-aleck about it. His whole demeanor changed into someone I didn't recognize, and he threw me across the room. Then he ran from the room. It was the only time he touched me in anger.

I believe there was a direct connection between the traumas he held so tightly inside himself and those post-war "not himself" experiences.

I recall, as a seventh grader, I got all caught up in the glory of war as I had seen it portrayed in John Wayne movies. One day, I asked him, "Hey, Dad, how many Germans did you kill in the war?" He looked me straight in the eye and, in a flat tone, answered, "None, I hope."

This was the same man who taught me how to capture an insect in the house and set it free unharmed back outside. "It wasn't trying to hurt us," he'd say, "so why should we hurt it?" Perhaps this was how he coped with unspeakable things. I will never know.

I tell of Dad because his war experience is, frankly, the best way I know to explain the difference between thin and thick stories. Stories that involved his trauma were told thinly, if at all. The only exception was the "I saw God" story that he so quickly cut off. He told other stories with detail and with humor—usually self-deprecating humor. I will never know what he felt on that Anzio beach or the degree of terror he felt as he waited for that grenade to kill him. But those things and likely many more unspoken ones affected this insect-rescuer to his core.

Recently, I talked with a man who counsels veterans. He told me the story of an aging World War II veteran. For several sessions, the vet described his combat experiences in the South Pacific. One day, the man was considerably more quiet than normal. When the counselor asked about that, the vet teared up and replied, "I'm trying to figure out whether I am a good man or a bad man." His rich telling of his experience had brought his war experiences back to the surface and had sparked in him a crisis of choosing between two thin meanings.

As we talk with people who have experienced a disaster, we are talking with persons who have been through their own war. Listening for thin stories and thick stories may well give us substantial clues about where their trauma is stored. We cannot become their therapists. We are, instead, Disaster Spiritual Care providers, and they are in our care for that purpose alone. They may be the ones who look heavenward, hoping to see God. While with them, we seek to be the enfleshed presence of this God they seek.

Having said that, however, there are some important insights that Disaster Spiritual Care providers can borrow from a type of therapy called Narrative Therapy. One very key one comes from narrative therapist Alice Morgan.

She describes narrative therapy as an approach that "seeks to be a respectful, non-blaming approach to counseling and community work, which centers people as the experts in their own lives. It views problems as separate from people and assumes people have many skills, competencies, beliefs, values, commitments, and abilities that will assist them to reduce the influence of problems in their lives" (Morgan, http://dulwichcentre.com.au/what-is-narrative-therapy).

Morgan notes the difference between "thin descriptions" and "thick descriptions" in the stories people tell about the problems they face. She notes that a thin description

> allows little space for the complexities and contradictions of life. It allows little space for people to articulate their own particular meanings of their actions and the context within which they occurred...Thin description often leads to thin conclusions about people's identities, and these have many negative effects...These thin conclusions, drawn from problem-saturated stories, disempower people as they are regularly based in terms of weaknesses, disabilities, dysfunctions or inadequacies (Morgan, http://dulwichcentre.com.au/what-is-narrative-therapy/).

Thin stories and the conclusions drawn from them are fertile and easy ground in which to grow even more thin stories. As the Katrina recovery was going on, some public media (both regionally and nationally) continued to reinforce the thin story that described Katrina as an "act of God." But some were not using the term as shorthand but rather as a description of God's judgment. Thus, the divine punishment explanation kept being reinforced by the "act of God" description. Many clung to it for perhaps no more reason than that it added up. It offered an explanation. Most importantly, it brought some temporary order into the chaos. In the face of all that, many of the volunteers who came to assist in the recovery bore posters asserting that "Katrina was an act of nature. Volunteers are an act of God." This re-framing sought to thicken the story of Katrina and open a door to the possibility of divine grace and love.

We can listen for thin stories, and they can become a pointer to where the trauma is. But we need also to keep in mind that, as we hear a thin story, it can only ever be a pointer. It is, in the end, a very subjective call. Allow for the fact that this person may be telling thin stories simply because he or she is exhausted or maybe always talks this way. Thin stories are pointers and always need to be heard as such.

Avoiding the Quick Fix: Meaning Making

People become disaster responders in order to relieve human suffering. It is a high calling, but seeking a quick fix to trauma is simply impossible. The goal of care is integration, not exorcism. Integration requires time and the knowledgeable guidance of one trained and prepared to be that guide. And it requires a sensitivity to the difference between thin and thick stories.

This is where the amygdala comes back into play. The amygdala is about reaction, not reason. When the amygdala becomes focused on helping us recognize and escape a threat, it has no time (or ability) to work with thickly thoughtful stories. But there is a way to weaken its grip.

One of the key books of the twentieth century was written by Holocaust survivor Viktor Frankl. It is called *Man's Search for Meaning*. Frankl, an Austrian Jew, was a neurologist and psychologist prior to being imprisoned by the Nazis at Auschwitz in 1944 with his wife Tilly. Later, he was transferred to Dachau. Tilly was moved to Bergen-Belsen, where she died. Viktor remained at Dachau until that camp was liberated in 1945 by the Allies. He had been put to work by the Nazis as a physician and therapist, but he also spent long months doing hard labor. He saw unspeakable tragedy.

Following his release, he spent intense days composing an account of his time in Dachau and Auschwitz. His writings later became the basis for his celebrated book. The theme of his book was that life has meaning. But one must find and embrace this meaning in order to survive. Much of the early part of his book focuses on how only the concentration camp prisoners who felt they had a purpose to their lives, a goal or future to live for, survived. "Everything," he wrote, "can be taken from a man but one thing: the last of the human freedoms—to choose one's attitude in any given set of circumstances, to choose one's own way" (Frankl, 1992, p. 62). He added, "Those who have a 'why' to live, can bear with almost any 'how'" (Frankl, 1992, p. 71). Janoff-Bulman noted, "Frankl experienced the shattering of two out of three fundamental assumptions about life— one, that the world is benevolent and two, that justice or fairness prevails" (Janoff-Bulman, 1992, pp. 6-12).

Psychologist Dan McAdams observed that, "whereas Frankl's ideas derived from a singular historical moment involving countless perpetrators and millions of victims, there is a sense in which psychologists' thinking about the reconstruction of meaning after trauma resembles, for each individual life, the Holocaust writ small" (McAdams & Jones, "Making Meaning in the Wake of Trauma: Resilience and Redemption", 2015).

On her website, Elizabeth Altmaier asks (http://www. elizabethaltmaier.com/recon.php), "Can people make sense out of events that just don't make sense?" She answers, "Yes. Sense-making means to develop and build the right type of inner examination of the trauma that promotes personal growth. Sometimes inner examinations only serve to re-inflict the trauma, and the person re-experiences the pain and horror over and over again. But sense making, in contrast, builds a story, a narrative, which is meaningful and causes life change" (Altmaier, "About Reconstructing Meaning after Trauma"). In other words, we often can't make sense of a disaster, but we can make sense of its meaning in life.

In sense-making or meaning-making, one struggles to develop a narrative sense out of the trauma experience. McAdams asks, "How do people make meaning in the wake of trauma? There are surely many viable answers to this question, but behind many of them is the supposition that meaning is made, in large part, through narrative" (McAdams & Jones, 2016, p. 5). This is the opening of the book to the "thick" story of the disaster and one's experience of it.

Keep the Book Open

This brings us again to one of the key responsibilities that we owe to those who have experienced disaster. Our time with them is limited, and, though we cannot engage in the therapy that someone might need, our job is to keep the book open for meaning-making. This sounds vague, and it is.

In a way, it is easier to describe closing the book. Closing the book happens when we (intentionally or unintentionally) send a message to the survivor that implies "you need to get on with it." An even more damaging book closing is when the caretaker's need to find a tidy resolution communicates that the survivor should pretend to be okay in order to meet that expectation.

We need always to keep in mind that there is an inherent imbalance of power when working with those who have experienced trauma. Survivors feel very powerless. They may be easily influenced by what they perceive to be the caregiver's ideas about how to proceed. What the caregiver intends as encouragement to find a way to move on from the disaster and live a newly-defined life may sound to them like, "Thin down your experience and hold it in. You've got to be strong." In that simple message we are unintentionally equating strength with holding everything in. What we really want to do is help them find the means to hold the book open for integrating their experience into the broad narrative of their lives, discover the strengths within themselves to hold on to hope, and even allow for the possibility of posttraumatic growth. This is the work of enfleshed presence.

Thin stories may be the "coin of the realm" for survivors in the early days after disaster, but our work includes helping them discover their resources for resiliency. We have a remarkable opportunity to help them hold that book open. Admittedly, just holding the book open may feel terribly incomplete. We truly want to see that survivor become well. But that can rarely happen in the early days and weeks. We are "book holders." This is an important part of recovery, yet it is still only a part. Each survivor has a blank last page in his or her life album. Our work is to assist them with recognizing it and not closing that album too soon.

Many clinicians believe that trauma never goes away. With time, however, its meaning can be integrated into one's life narrative in such a way as to make posttraumatic growth a possibility. In other words, trauma need not be the end of the story. There are more sentences to write. Resilience may be traced to what meaning a person can draw from his or her experience of the trauma and how that can, indeed, open pathways to personal growth. Professionals, family, and even communities can, over time, assist in facilitating that growth. It will take time, and we are unlikely to witness its resolution.

In the early hours and days following a disaster, we are focused on keeping that pathway open and realizing that, later on, others will almost certainly have to be their long-term guides. We keep in mind during those early hours and days *Primum non nocere*—"first, do no harm", derived from the Hippocratic Oath. That should be written in our hearts so that we can always be reminded of our mission, which is to avoid the harm caused by closing the book to that post-disaster integration.

It is important that every journey begins with a destination in mind and a plan to get there. Resiliency is the destination we wish for those we work with. But just what is resiliency, and how does the person in our care get there?

Summary

Humans are equipped with a remarkably efficient part of the brain called the amygdala. It quickly assesses threat and initiates protective measures. But it is very old fashioned and doesn't understand the modern world. Sometimes it stores trauma that the rest of the brain is ill-prepared to resolve. As responders, we are not therapists and should stay in our own lane and attend to the spiritual dimensions of disaster response. One valuable listening tool is to recognize the difference between "thick" and "thin" stories. Thin stories may be pointers to where trauma is stored. Thick stories are where the feelings are disclosed and "pat" answers are avoided. We focus instead on keeping open avenues for hope, resiliency, and recovery.

Preview

Let's now take a closer look at resiliency and the obstacles that may block a person's journey there.

4
The Red Rubber Ball of Resiliency

And What to Do When Things Don't Add Up

And I think it's gonna be all right
Yeah, the worst is over now
The mornin' sun is shinin' like a red rubber ball

(Simon & Woodley, "Red Rubber Ball", 1966)

Back in 1966, The Cyrkle recorded a hit song, "Red Rubber Ball." The song is sung from the perspective of one who has just been jilted by the young woman he loved. But the chorus shines light on the young man's resilience: "And I think it's gonna be all right/Yeah, the worst is over now/The mornin' sun is shinin' like a red rubber ball."

All disaster responders aim to put a red rubber ball in the sky of those they serve. Whether it be rebuilding infrastructures, homes, businesses, or lives, resiliency is the goal. *The Merriam-Webster Dictionary* defines resiliency as "the ability to recover from or adjust easily to misfortune or change." Most responders would take issue with the word "easily" in that definition. When someone has lost a large part of everything, resiliency is not easy. It is doggone hard. And for many in the early days or months after such a loss, recovery may seem impossible. This is true for damaged buildings, homes, and businesses. But it is also true—perhaps especially true—for damaged lives.

As I mentioned earlier, the phrase "new normal" is now frequently used to describe the fruit of recovery following a disaster. But, as I noted, the term may be misleading to some because it leaves open the idea that the new life will somehow resemble the old life. For many, "new normal" will be quite unlike the pre-disaster life. But the term does acknowledge that things can't ever be exactly the same again, and that something new is now the goal. It forecasts that the

45

new will become the normal eventually. Things will be different in so many ways, even including how the survivors understand themselves. This "new" happens through the integration of the disaster experiences into one's Narrative Identity, as meaning replaces chaos.

What can "new normal" possibly mean for those who have experienced significant trauma? It is quite hard to look to a brighter future when a darker past has embedded itself deeply into someone like a tick on a dog. There are losses to mourn, challenges to face, confusions to work through, and uncertainties to come to grips with. And one cannot even begin to think about those things until basic needs of food, water, safety, and shelter for themselves and their loved ones have been met and taken root.

Resilient People

Having noted the difficulty, it is important to note something else quite important about resiliency. Research has shown that resilience to even great trauma is surprisingly common. Research psychologist George Bonanno speculates that as many as 40 to 50 percent of trauma survivors may exhibit a resilience trajectory. Hard figures are difficult to come by since many resilient people do not consult helpers following their trauma. They seem to tough out the early stages and then attain new stability after a while. Some even experience posttraumatic growth. As McAdams notes, "newfound personal strengths or enhanced interpersonal relationships or a renewed sense of spirituality may arise, suggesting that positive, growth-inducing meanings have been made" (McAdams & Jones, "Making Meaning in the Wake of Trauma: Resilience and Redemption", 2016).

Resiliency, though, does not imply ease. Resilient people are not necessarily free of pain and suffering. But they have an arsenal of coping weapons that, as McAdams suggests, includes:

- High levels of social support

- Personality dispositions that reinforce a sense of hardiness
- A tendency to engage in self-enhancement
- An ability to trigger and savor positive emotions
- A repressive coping style (McAdams & Jones, "Making Meaning in the Wake of Trauma: Resilience and Redemption", 2016)

The last one is quite interesting. Though repressing feelings and emotions is often predictive of difficulty, it is also often associated with those who may be called resilient. Some researchers contend that for naturally resilient people, traumatic events do not shatter assumptions or force them into a protracted season of intense grieving or distress. They show relatively minor and fleeting disruptions in their ability to function. "Resilient individuals may experience transient perturbations in normal functioning (e.g., several weeks of sporadic preoccupation or restless sleep) but generally exhibit a stable trajectory of healthy functioning across time, as well as the capacity for generative experiences and positive emotions" (Bonanno, 2004, p. 21).

The implication is that not all persons we meet in the early days following a disaster will remain trapped in their trauma. Upwards of half of them will be okay whether we provide care to them or not. Our care, though, may hasten recovery for them, but recovery will not be finally determined by it. This suggests how important it is for us to avoid pathologizing those we serve and keep ourselves focused on the inner strengths and resources they have available. This works equally well for naturally resilient people and for those with less resilient natures.

I note this because, in the adrenaline-driven early response, it may be easy to slip into thinking that our effectiveness will be measured by how well the disaster-affected person responds to our care. That is much too big of a burden to bear. And it is a burden that blurs the goals and objectives of early response. Our work is not to somehow make a person well. It is to help them hold open a book to well-being. They will use their own resources to initiate their meaning-making and initiating the journey back to a life marked by "well-being." That is quite enough of a mission in and of itself.

However...

Even if Bonanno's estimate that up to half of all people are resilient in the face of trauma, that still leaves that other half. There seems no doubt that many disaster survivors do lose faith in the benevolence of the world, the world's meaningfulness, and/or the worthiness of the self (remember Janoff-Bulman). Put another way, the sacred story carried deep within has been severely challenged or destroyed.

Years ago, Stephen Crites proposed that there are two kinds of stories that shape us. The first form he called "mundane stories." These are the stories we tell and may record in books or journals. They are our best efforts to bring to the conscious mind the second form, which he calls "sacred stories." He writes,

> People do not sit down on a cool afternoon and think themselves up a sacred story. They awaken to a sacred story, and their most significant mundane stories are told in the effort, never fully successful, to articulate it. For the sacred story does not transpire within a conscious world. It forms the very consciousness that projects a total world horizon, and therefore informs the intentions by which actions are projected into that world (Crites, 1971, p. 296).

He adds that he calls these "...sacred stories, not so much because gods are commonly celebrated in them, but because men's [one's] sense of self and world is created through them" (Crites, 1971, p. 295).

Jim and Mary

Jim and Mary Jones were members of a congregation that I served years ago. They were not disaster survivors, but their story illustrates Crites' description of sacred and mundane stories.

Jim was muscular and handsome. Mary had a kind of presence that drew people to her. They had met years earlier on a public beach. He was a lifeguard, she a frequent swimmer.

He was tender and giving in relationships and seemed genuinely interested in other people and was held in high respect by those who knew him. Quiet and reflective, he had a natural smile and was comfortable to be with.

She, too, was sensitive and caring. She created a pleasant glow in others—a glow that remained even after she had left the room. She had high energy and the ability to catch others up into it. Sounds like the beginning of a fairy tale, right?

One day Mary came to me with the surprising news that she and Jim were divorcing. I was astonished because they seemed to be such a happy couple—she was bouncy, and he smiling. She claimed that she just couldn't take him anymore, that he was a weakling and a panderer. Later, in talking with Jim, he complained that she was always trying to start an argument and that he was fed up.

Their complaints were contrary to the way that I knew each of them. I had always sensed Jim as sensitive and strong. I knew her as easy to get along with. Their troubles didn't add up. After talking with them a few times, I knew that there was much more to this than his wishy-washy ways and her argumentativeness. There were two world views, sacred stories, if you will, in conflict.

He had grown up in a home where his parents never fought in front of the children. She had grown up in a home where her mother and father fought constantly and eventually divorced. Their early lives had woven into each of them an understanding of how relationships work and how they don't. And those understandings could not have been more different.

She had told of watching the TV show "Father Knows Best" while growing up. She said she watched in order to see how real families got along. She internalized how a solid father is supposed to be. Jim watched that same TV show and, strengthened by his own home experience, simply accepted as normative a home where no one ever dared allow conflict. Each day of their childhood and adolescence had served to weave within them these conflicting sacred stories of how families work and, for that matter, how life itself should work.

This was the dilemma in which Jim and Mary Jones found themselves entangled. Fortunately, despite the fact that I had not yet discovered sacred stories, they survived my counseling and worked these things out without much effective help from me.

Kadel's Law of Sacred Stories

Some years later I became trained in family systems therapy, and I left parish ministry for a few years to became a partner in a family therapy practice. I worked with a number of couples who were in conflict. Many of them struggled with the same issue as Jim and Mary—warring sacred stories. What struck me on a regular basis was that, when I spoke with each partner alone, I had the sense that they were describing their relationship as honestly as possible. Yet, their individual descriptions were often worlds apart. The stories didn't add up. Recalling Crites, I developed something that I began to call "Kadel's Law." This "law" went like this: "when things don't add up, you are treading on sacred turf." Initially, this was simply a bit of wisdom to guide me in my work with those couples. When the stories didn't add up, I needed to dig deeper with them. At some level, nearer the sacred story level, things would add up. Kadel's Law was a big help to me.

I had no idea back then that Kadel's Law would also—and perhaps even more so—assist me in working with people who had experienced a disaster.

Perhaps conceptualizing one's sacred story as an intricate yet unseen tapestry of life-learnings offers a useful image. Consider this fictionalized story of Susan. Susan grew up and had lived her life according to a sacred story that, if put inadequately into words, would go something like this: "If you try to live a good life and treat people fairly and respectfully, life will add up." It will, of course, have many twists and turns, but her sacred story asserted that a well-lived life will yield a well-loved life. Good will come of being good.

But one day, a tornado stormed through Susan's little hometown. It wreaked massive destruction. Tornado warnings had been sounded and the couple took their children to their basement for shelter. They seemed as safe as possible. But Susan's husband was killed when their children began to cry for their beloved family dog Bootsy. He knew better, but he still rushed out of their basement to try to rescue the dog. He and Bootsy didn't make it back. And to layer tragedy upon tragedy, Susan's house was destroyed by the savage wind. She and her two little children somehow survived. But practically nothing was left of her life. It lay in ruins amidst the rubble of their house. "How can this be?" she cried out. "Why?"

And though her rational mind tried to make sense of all this tragedy, it could not overpower her sacred story that "good will come of being good." She desperately needed to find relief from the chaos that had descended upon her. She knew perfectly well that tornadoes are unpredictable and that her husband had made a bad choice, but that couldn't answer why the storm had singled her and her family out. She could not make her sacred story stop its screaming. Chaos was everywhere in their little town, but nothing matched the chaos she experienced inside herself. Her assumptions were shattered, but all she could feel was a painful hole in her soul.

Let's remind ourselves of some things I mentioned back in the introduction. It has been my observation that we humans cannot tolerate chaos for long. We are driven to create order. And if no other answers are available to do that, people will often create what we will call thin stories in the effort to do it. The stories do not have to be based on fact or even be rational. They only have to answer the question of "Why?" In the short term, sometimes these stories will, indeed, sustain them and give some order amidst their chaos. In the longer term, however, their new mundane stories may only bring more misery. This is where the image of a tapestry can be useful. A disaster brings chaos and, in effect, tears a hole in the fabric of our understanding of how life is supposed to work. We cannot see the tear, but we can feel it.

In the days following the tornado, Susan sought some kind of "something" that would make her losses add up. She thought of the argument she had had with her husband only hours before the tornado and how she angrily shouted "You idiot!" when he left to find the dog. Maybe this was her punishment for becoming so angry. She thought of one failure after another after another in her life until the sheer bulk of her failings began to add up to the scale of this punishment. She had been a flawed person. Now she was flawed, widowed, and homeless. This thin story worked to bring order to the chaos but left a time bomb in her heart.

In the days after the tornado, Susan had trouble accepting assistance because something inside her kept telling her she didn't deserve it. This, connected with her grieving, sent her into emotional and physical isolation. As time went on, she became harder and harder on her children, and, if she had been able to put it into words, she would have said that she wanted to train them not to be as flawed as she was—so that they would not experience painful issues later in their lives. Of course, it had the opposite effect on her children.

Something in her kept telling her that none of this was rational. Yet, that voice had the lesser volume. Recall Janoff-Bulman's notion of holding within us a schema and how a schema is so very hard to undo. But in Susan's case, the sheer weight of the thin story she had adopted not only conflicted with her schema but also created a brand new and powerful alternative schema: I am flawed, and this causes suffering. This alternative schema had become woven into and radically modified her original sacred story. The chaos of Susan's circumstance cried out for some kind of order—any kind of order. Blaming the tornado on her own failings added up. It provided a cause-and-effect framework that gave her some sense of order—even if it was the most painful kind of order possible. The need for order from chaos became expressed inside of her as that story, one that explained why things were the way they were.

Susan was simply doing what so many others have done – seeking order in the midst of chaos. Everything in us seeks order – a narrative or story that explains things. The key is that the thin story that may help us does not necessarily need to reflect fact. It only needs to bring some sense of release from chaos.

We noted the thin story that Hurricane Katrina was an "act of God." But there is more to that story. Almost immediately after the great storm, very public voices tried to supply this sense of order. Less than two weeks after the hurricane, Pat Robertson implied in the September 12 broadcast of The 700 Club that the hurricane was God's punishment in response to America's abortion policy. He further suggested that 9/11 and the disaster in New Orleans "could... be connected in some way." Robertson was also credited (falsely) with a statement that God sent Hurricane Katrina as punishment for the selection of openly gay Ellen DeGeneres to host the Emmy Awards. Though it apparently was rooted in a satirical Dateline Hollywood article, even it got traction with parts of the public for a while.

New Orleans attorney Jesse Grisham formed an organization called People Against Natural Disasters that filed a lawsuit against the Vatican claiming "that insufficient and inadequate prayers to God for protection is partly to blame for the increasing number of people being killed, injured, and displaced by acts of God." And there were other voices that made similar claims. Even Al Qaeda in Iraq declared that, through Katrina, "God attacked America, and the prayers of the oppressed were answered" (Dyson, 2005, p. 183). Of course, absent from all of these claims was the fact that the French Quarter of New Orleans was largely unaffected. So, "when things don't add up, you are treading on sacred turf."

Nothing about the Katrina claims added up or even resonated remotely with either the facts of the storm or the basic religious texts of the claiming parties. But each of these and so many others drew believers. Why? The claims—as varied as they were—provided an explanation: this was God's work. That explanation was repeated in many ways. But it was repeated. The stories were told and re-told. It helped make things add up for many people—at least for a while. As order began to be restored to the Gulf Coast, we heard fewer and fewer of these kinds of claims. They were not so necessary as time wore on. Order was coming from elsewhere.

In truth, I myself relied on stories in Katrina's aftermath. I was in coastal Mississippi days after the hurricane. At one point, I was involved in delivering a large shipment of food and supplies to the Vietnamese community in Biloxi. The food had been gathered and shipped by a Jewish synagogue in Cleveland, Ohio, received by a Lutheran Church in Ocean Springs, Mississippi, and distributed by a Buddhist Temple in Biloxi. "Only God could have thought that one up" was how I ended my oft-repeated telling of that story. It helped me make sense of God's involvement in that great suffering. We all do it. Stories—including thin ones—are the language of disaster aftermath. Mundane stories interpret sacred stories. Thin, mundane stories, though, may very well put us on a difficult path.

Meaning, Not Sense

Kadel's Law can be a helpful thing when we talk with disaster survivors in near-term recovery. As we listen to those we care for, we keep in mind a question: do their stories add up or do they leave us feeling puzzled or confused? We should pay attention to any confused or puzzled feelings. They may be alerting us to something.

"Adding up" is different than "making meaning." The need to bring order from chaos so often results in those thin "adding up" stories that can be harmful later on. And though we cannot deny that some people can cling to thin stories for a very long time (perhaps a lifetime), they will dead-end for the majority at some point.

Most trauma experts suggest that it is a far better thing to point survivors toward discovering the meaning that their experience and its trauma may hold for them. Some call this a "redemptive narrative." It aims toward an eventual resolution that leaves the person with new insights or strengths. "Psychological adaption tends to be positively associated with the extent to which people feel that they own and control their own memories, rather than feeling owned or controlled by the memories themselves" (Crone & Beike, 2012, p. 279). When one feels owned by the memories, the strong urge is to resolve that as quickly as possible, and that is what can give rise to those thin stories.

As we remember our role and stay in our lane, we take all of this in, but we do not try to become the survivor's therapist. In that case, what is the point of listening for thin and thick stories and being aware of when things don't add up? Our limited role in the survivor's life is a critical but not final factor. When we have a sense of the outcome we wish for, it becomes much clearer how to assist that survivor with holding the book open for eventual resolution. The very act of holding the book open is what we call hope.

Summary

Studies indicate that upward of half the population may be naturally resilient people. Their path following disaster may contain grief and difficulty, but they will eventually be whole again by virtue of their own inner "workings." The remainder of survivors, though, may require assistance. This assistance may begin, but will not end, with DSC responders. We listen for things in another person's story that don't add up and use those things as pointers to guide them through our care—always knowing that others may have to follow them on the long-term path of caregiving. We do not seek to resolve trauma but instead to keep the book open to additional pages, which, hopefully, may help that person discover new hope-fueled meaning for their lives.

Preview

In a fictitious account of Nikki and her DSC responder, Tracey, we will discover insights into the nature of one survivor's resiliency and how, in non-threatening ways, the book was kept open for her. We will encounter the powerful idea of identifying a personal creedal statement.

5

When Beauty Became a Creed

"There is no greater agony than bearing an untold story inside you."

– Maya Angelou

This is a fictitious story that describes a certain Disaster Spiritual Care responder named Tracey caring for a flood survivor named Nikki. Neither of these people actually exists, but they both exist in many people with whom we will work. Notice the notations A, B, C, etc. These indicate key points in the conversation. Following the dialogue, I'll describe those key points.

A Conversation in a Shelter

Nikki sat on her cot in the bustling shelter, staring blankly into space. Her face was painted with a thousand-yard stare. It was now two days after the rain started in Smithton, Arkansas. The flood waters had forced Nikki and her two young daughters out of their modest home. They remained in the community shelter at Rock Valley High School. Word was the waters were receding, but the forecast for later this day included even more rain. The few belongings they left the house with were stashed under their cots. Official information about the condition of their home and the others in the same flooded part of town was scarce. But that didn't stop the conjectures that spread among those in the shelter. The most common view was that all houses in that part of town had been severely damaged and would be unlivable until repaired. All that any of them could know for sure was that they couldn't go home.

Nikki's blank stare snapped away when she noticed a woman in a vest that read "Spiritual Care". The woman seemed to stop at many cots and talk with people. Nikki was not in the mood to talk with anyone—especially about God. She wasn't even sure there was a God; surely this disaster had weakened even that thin connection.

When she saw the woman in the vest heading her way, she looked for a way to avoid her, but she seemed stuck.

The woman in the vest finally reached her. She identified herself as Tracey Hawkins, a Disaster Spiritual Care responder from some organization Nikki had never heard of. "Hello," she said. "May I speak with you for a few moments?"

"Well, okay," Nikki said, caution in her voice. She had spoken with a number of these "helpers" already. Talk wasn't going to fix anything. Tracey seated herself on a nearby empty cot and initiated conversation, asking if she needed anything. "I'm fine, thank you," Nikki answered flatly. (A)

"Nikki," Tracey asked, "can you help me better understand what has happened to you? What have these past days have been like for you?" (B)

Nikki began to tell her story. It included watching the weather reports and the warnings that flooding was possible. She told about trying to keep her children busy in their "rainy day" boredom, but how she kept one eye on the weather outside and one ear pealed to the local TV station's updates on the storm. The TV warnings kept getting more dire, and her worries kept growing.

Suddenly there was a knock on her door. It was a police officer. He spoke to her in polite but firm tones. "Ma'am, I am Officer Dan Templeton from the Smithton Police Department. A mandatory evacuation has been declared for this part of town. The river is rising quickly, and there's a good chance that it will flood this low-lying neighborhood. Please, quickly gather your family, any medicines you use, and leave your house. If you have no place to go, you may go to the high school where a shelter is being set up. This is for your safety, ma'am. They will have things that you need there like food and shelter. I'm sorry, but this is not optional."

With that, the officer turned and headed to the next house.

"A hundred things went through my mind at the same time," Nikki continued, noticeably more animated. "I had to figure out what to take. What clothes do my daughters need? Can I take books and games to keep them occupied? What will happen to my house? How long will this be?"

"Teach me what this was like for you," Tracey asked. (C)

"I was pretty confused and scared, I guess." Nikki responded as if the question had startled her. "Is that what you want to know?"

"What were you most scared about?"

"My girls, my house, my stuff—I worried about it all."

"What did you do with all of that worry? What worries you most right now?" (D)

"Oh, I don't know. I just did what was necessary to get us safe. I guess I've been thinking about my ex and what he would have said if he were here."

"What do you mean?"

"I'm not very good at taking care of things. He used to hammer me with that all the time. I was sure that I'd screw up somehow. I'm a screw-up."

"Is that what he called you—a screw-up?" (E)

"All the time."

"What do you think will happen when the water goes back down?" (F)

"If the house is ruined, I don't know what I'll do. I'll never be able to take care of that. Where will we go? How can I get my girls through whatever it is we need to get through? How is school going to happen? I can't imagine how this will work out. I'm not good at this." (G)

After a long pause, Nikki continued. "You have Spiritual Care on your vest? Do you think God caused this flood?" (H)

"That sounds like a very big question, Nikki. For now, let's just say that I believe that God has me here for you." (I)

"Thank you. It is hard being alone through all of this. This is hard."

"That's what I am hearing from everyone here. I can't imagine how this could be anything but hard," Tracey replied. (J) "There's a lot of not-so-great stuff happening to you right now. I wonder if you can even think of anything beautiful at this point?" (K)

"I suppose I've always thought sunrises were beautiful."

"What is it about the beauty of a sunrise that affects you so deeply?" Tracey asked. (L)

After some thought, Nikki answered, "I guess it just points to the fact that good things *can* exist."

"When else have good things existed for you?" (M)

"My daughters. In the birth of my daughters. Can't think of anything else right now."

"You gave birth to beauty, you mean?" (N)

"I guess I did."

"What else have you given beautiful birth to? I wonder what beautiful births are ahead for you." (O)

The conversation lasted only a few moments more. But Tracey's final question could be called the "keep the book open" question.

Notes on Tracey's Conversation with Nikki

(A) Tracey's first concern was for this family's physical needs. But as Tracey had approached Nikki, she noticed the "thousand-yard stare" on her face. This was a phrase that was initially used to describe battle weary soldiers; Tracey also knew that it was a signal of dissociation for disaster survivors as well. It is an effect that disaster responders take seriously. It may indicate that this person is quite deeply affected by trauma— possibly in shock. It is necessary to proceed especially carefully.

(B) Tracey continues with another question that allows Nikki to enter the conversation at whatever level she chooses. This allows Nikki to share what she is comfortable

60

with—from a dispassionate log of events to a full description of the emotional toll the events have required of her. This question helps Nikki begin to put time back into the sequence of past, present, and future. This simple step can help her more reliably use her natural cognitive processes. Tracey's question also sends the message that no one can truly know what this or any other survivor has been through. Tracey was careful not to seem to probe into things that may, for now, be too difficult for Nikki to think about.

(C) Tracey's question is framed in such a way as to lessen the "power" imbalance with Nikki. By asking her to "teach," Tracey is putting Nikki in the driver's seat and allowing her to enter the story at whatever point she wants and with whatever degree of detail Nikki is ready to share. "Teach me" is an empowering request.

(D) Tracey continues to assist Nikki with placing her concerns in a priority order by asking about her here-and-now concerns. It is okay to ask more than one question at a time. This gives Nikki the opportunity to choose which question to answer.

(E) Tracey attempts to separate Nikki from her label as a screw-up. By attaching the label to her former husband, she is able to begin this process.

(F) Tracey checks on Nikki's expectations for the future. She is still assisting Nikki with sorting out past, present, and future. Now, for those future expectations.

(G) Tracey takes note of Nikki's concern about screwing up but is also aware that Nikki has done a good job at getting herself and her daughters into the shelter. Tracey makes a mental note that Nikki's view of her ability and what she has already done doesn't "add up." For the first time in that conversation, Nikki mentions her daughters and her concern for them. Her worry about getting her daughters *through this disaster is part of a larger sense of wanting to help them through a whole range of difficult life situations, and it illuminates a substantial degree of connection with them.*

(H) Nikki attempts to change the subject. However, Tracey notes that this question is an expression of another thin story. Thin stories typically look for simple reasons and causes. Most of us are driven to establish order in the chaos of our broken expectations of how the world works. But, as we said, while this may provide some comfort in the short term, Nikki may need Tracy's assistance to keep the book open to the thicker ones. Also notice that Tracey resisted the temptation to fill up the long pause. It is always best not to try to fill silences with words just for the sake of reducing the caretaker's own anxiety.

(I) Tracey knows nothing about Nikki's spiritual beliefs and practices. She avoids getting into a theological discussion. Instead, she re-frames her question into something that doesn't put Nikki on the spot or expect her to modify or change her own spirituality. The hours, days, and weeks after a disaster are not teachable moments. But Tracey also frames her response in a way that affirms her own spirituality without making it something that Nikki must agree with. While this is not the time for Tracey to teach Nikki any doctrinal viewpoints about God, it is a moment to name something vital. Spiritual Care is about enfleshed presence. This important kind of presence should never be underestimated. It is very powerful. For now, rather than try to teach Nikki about a God who is always present, she will simply point it out by saying that she, the Spiritual Care person, is there. If later Nikki opens that book wider by asking more specific questions about God, Tracey will be ready to respond with her own affirmation of God being present and concerned for all of them. But for now, Tracey recognizes that she can help Nikki experience a God-

presence through her own presence and the way she listens to Nikki's life story.

(J) It is reasonable for this experience to be very difficult for everyone. Tracey is trying to "normalize" Nikki's feelings. Nikki is describing a normal response to an abnormal experience. Tracey works to give Nikki a sense that her reactions are typical in these circumstances.

(K) Tracey does not want to place Nikki in the position of having to share a deeper and more emotionally thick recounting about what she has been through. Recalling that thousand-yard stare and the possibility of Nikki being in shock, Tracey wants to avoid any chance of re-traumatizing Nikki. If Nikki is ready to share this, that information will come. Tracey's response not only continues to affirm the normality of Nikki's response but also adds a new image, beauty, into the conversation. Notice that Tracey asks the question in an open-ended way—avoiding the pathway to a thin "yes" or "no" response.

(L) Tracey is working nimbly to assist Nikki with finding her inner resources that can become key in her recovery. She is shifting the focus from ugliness to beauty.

(M) Tracey offers Nikki a safe way to access her inner resources. And she asks her question out of a genuine interest. She doesn't know what good things have been a part of Nikki's life. Genuine interest is vital in this kind of conversation. People in Nikki's circumstance are likely to be quite sensitive to manipulation.

(N) Tracey re-frames the beauty subject and applies it to the fact that this one who considers herself a screw-up is one who has created beauty already.

(O) Note how Tracey ties two questions together. The first connects her observation that she has given birth to beauty before and opens the door for her to consider other times she has given birth to beautiful. The second builds on that and

looks to the future—that symbolic empty last page that awaits the new beautiful births. Tracey is not asking contrived questions. Her questions are sincere and natural. They encourage Nikki to take the lead in remembering that she has given birth to beauty—the exact inner resource that she will need to lead her family's recovery from this flood. From there it is not an unnatural leap to wonder how she can use those resources after the flood. Recovery, then, becomes a thing of beauty. That is an expression of spirituality. But it is more. It is a creedal statement upon which hope can be born. Beauty sustains hope, and hope is the necessary element in recovery. The creedal statement itself could be "I believe I can give birth to a beautiful future with my daughters."

Nikki would not have gotten to that creedal statement had Tracey initially asked her directly, "What is your expectation for the future?" Now that a type of creedal ("I believe") statement has formed for her, it may be a good time for Tracey to ask about her expectations for the future. When Nikki connected the idea of beauty with her daughters, she identified a narrative that can embolden her.

Note also that Tracey did not directly confront Nikki's Narrative Identity of being a screw-up. That would have met with impossible resistance. Schemas, remember, are very difficult to change. Instead, Tracey allowed the rejected idea (that Nikki is a capable person) to become the beginning of an alternative schema ("I've given birth to beauty before; I can do it again.") The stone that the builder rejected can now become the cornerstone. In this brief conversation, Nikki has come from believing herself to be only a screw-up to entertaining the notion that she is one who has given birth to beauty before and can do it again.

Tracey led Nikki to embrace the alternative schema, form a creedal statement, and plant her very own seeds for hope. That is effective Disaster Spiritual Care—care led by the very story presented by the survivor. The book is open.

What Just Happened? Let's Go Over This Again!

It is important to keep in mind that no disaster survivor is a blank slate. Nikki's whole life is the canvas upon which the story of her recovery will be painted. This was clearly true for Nikki.

Note the subtle but powerful approach Tracey took after Nikki told of being labeled as a "screw-up" by her former husband. Tracey simply asked, "Is that what he called you—a screw-up?" Tracey's response was not to disagree with the former husband. That would only have met with resistance from Nikki and, likely, a rebuttal listing other times she had felt defeated by a problem. Instead, Tracey initiated a separation of Nikki from the label: "Is that what he called you?" Note the externalizing. Tracey's response is quite subtle, for sure, but often subtle is powerful. Screw-up is *his* label, not *her* identity. Tracey went on to explore the conclusions Nikki had drawn about her assumed future. "What do you think will happen when the water goes back down?" Nikki's answer brought the true issue to full bloom. "If the house is ruined, I don't know what I'll do. I'll never be able to take care of that. Where will we go?"

Tracey heard these things in their conversation. Her first effort was to separate Nikki as a person from the problems and worries deep within her. This is called externalizing the problem. Tracey will subtly rephrase Nikki's statement ("I am a screw-up") into "You have been called a screw-up." Whenever possible, Tracey will externalize this by retelling parts of Nikki's story in slightly different ways. She could also have said, "Screw-up sounds like a very heavy load to carry in your bag." Or "It sounds like 'screw-up' may have tricked you into believing that's all you do."

Describing herself as a screw-up is a "thin" story. It is thin because it is a label that had been fixed upon her by an abusive partner, and it opened the door for her belief that she cannot effectively attend to the well-being of her girls and herself. It is also thin because it is a simplistic view of herself that fails to acknowledge the complexity of life and the complexity of the problems that life poses. It ignores what she has already done. It is simplistic because, through it, she portrays herself as a shadowy, passive, and ineffective player even in her own life. There is no evidence-based hope for the future in her self-narrative.

Flood Is Not the Main Thing

Tracey has helped Nikki get to the heart of things. The flood waters are not the main thing for her. She is living out a thin story in which she sees herself as an incompetent screw-up. For Nikki, the flood is just the stage upon which her incompetence will be exposed and will cause damage to the daughters she loves. Still missing from everything Nikki has told about so far are the substantial efforts she took to assure her daughters' safety and well-being. Likewise, there was no reference to how she had handled her own safety. These things were nowhere in Nikki's story. Nikki had been stuck in a thin story.

Tracey noticed not only the thin description that Nikki used of herself but also the lack of positives. Her story didn't add up. Whatever Nikke has accomplished by successfully coping with problems in the past is now quite hidden from her. What hope would a total "screw-up" have for recovering from a devastating flood, much less helping two young daughters do the same?

In this brief exchange, Nikki has begun to offer Tracey what we will call a story map of how to care for her. Tracey's goal is not to convert Nikki to any particular belief system. Rather, it is to assist Nikki with holding open the possibility that she might discover two vital things—power and connection—or to introduce two new and important terms, agency and communion. We will look more deeply into agency and communion shortly. Of all the many things Nikki will need in order to have hope for life *before* death, these two may be the most vital. They are the keystones to hope. Hope is that "thing" that opens a pathway to recovery—not a recovery of the way things used to be but a recovery of a life with a sufficient sense of meaning that it is more than survivable. It is life before death. Perhaps Nikki may even experience posttraumatic growth. That book, that hope, must remain open.

As in many cases of disaster response, this may be the one and only time Tracey will talk with Nikki. This initial (and brief) conversation has focused on two important tasks. First, Tracey wants to open up Nikki's own resources for discovering her possibilities, no matter how unspecific those possibilities may initially be. Tracey is guiding Nikki into uncovering helpful ways for her to think about herself as a competent person who has already demonstrated that she has within her what it takes to forge a new life for herself and her daughters. In other words, her goal is to assist Nikki to thicken her self-story. Tracey worked at this by being an enfleshed presence with her.

What Tracey Did

Please note also that Tracey did not attempt to become Nikki's therapist. Nikki may later choose to deal with the "screw-up" identity imposed upon her by her former husband. And even though Tracey's time with her was short, she held the book open for that later consideration. For Nikki, this may prove to be a very valuable thing.

Note also that Tracey was very sensitive in assisting Nikki with identifying her own inner spirituality. Though not framed in traditional "God-talk," Tracey helped her embrace the idea of beauty and then apply that idea to earlier times of her life. If she has given beautiful birth before, she can do it again. Tracey helped Nikki form this into a powerful creedal statement: "I believe I can give birth to a beautiful future with my daughters."

Finally, Tracey sought to accomplish all of this without risking more trauma for Nikki. She did not try to pry into Nikki's experience of the flood and her reaction to it any more deeply than Nikki was comfortable going.

Throughout this conversation, Tracey was also making use of tools from the fields of Narrative Identity and Narrative Therapy and applying them to spiritual care.

Tracey had learned to listen with story-sensitive ears. She listened for Nikki's story and, in particular, listened for certain dynamics within it. Pointers in that story helped Tracey know how to proceed. If we remember back to how stories are created, we'll notice that Tracey paid careful attention to each period in Nikki's story and encouraged her to form a meaning-filled next sentence.

Summary

Nikki and her daughters have been displaced by flood waters. Tracey, a Disaster Spiritual Care responder, listens to her story as the enfleshed presence of God, gains a sense of Nikki's narrative understanding of herself, and begins to help her discover a path to keeping the book open to the possibility of additional "beautiful births" in her future.

Preview

In the next chapter, we will look at how to develop our own story ears. And we will find a quick and easy way to keep track of what we hear and to develop a story map with the ones we serve.

6

Narrative Listening

How to Have Story Ears

"You're short on ears and long on mouth."

— John Wayne, *Big Jake*, 1971

If I am asked, "Who are you?" there are a number of ways I might respond. The answer would depend upon the context within which the question was asked. If I am at a party and talking with someone I have never met before, I would likely answer simply, "My name is Tom." If asked at a meeting of disaster responders, my answer might be, "My name is Tom Kadel, and I am involved in Disaster Spiritual Care." But if the circumstance called for it, I may very well begin to tell a story of who I am. In the first two instances, I am giving information. If I tell a story of who I am, I draw on both the conscious and unconscious meaning of my life. I won't bore the other person with an account of everything I can remember about myself, but I'd tell a themed story that lifts up the meaning that I have for my life. We understand the meaning of our lives in story or narrative fashion, and that is how we'd tell it to others.

This common and quite natural kind of telling and hearing is the foundation for Narrative Listening. It can also be our best friend as we talk with people whose lives have been shattered by a disaster.

The Big Two

An important door was opened to understanding the narrative nature of how we understand our lives in 1966 by David Baken when he published a landmark book titled *The Duality of Human Existence* (Baken, 1966). In it, he proposed that there are two key factors in our understanding of ourselves and, by extension, others – agency and communion.

Agency refers to one's sense of individuation and an individual's sense of personal potency. It describes the functioning of an organism as an individual. Communion refers to one's sense of being part of something larger and to the strength of that connectedness. It describes the participation of a person as a part of some larger organism of which that individual is a part.

Soon enough research psychologists began to expand the concept to refer to thematic clusters in life narratives. The clusters articulate important life goals, striving, needs, and desires" (McAdams, "Coding Autobiographical Episodes for Themes of Agency and Communion", 2001 (r)). Since that time, agency and communion have been described as "the big two."

Since Baken, a growing number of researchers have focused on taking the narrative understanding of ourselves much more seriously. Narrative Identity has been the subject of considerable theorizing, research, and study. It suggests that individuals form an identity by integrating life experiences into an internalized and evolving story of the self, which yields a sense of unity, purpose, and meaning in life that can be discerned upon those scales of agency and communion. We hold versions of this narrative in both our unconscious and conscious levels. In other words, this is a narrative that asks if I believe that I can affect the course of my life and of the world around me. And, if I can, to what purpose will I affect it? How will it work out when I try? And who will be with me?

Narrative Identity concerns itself with a person's past, present, and imagined future, and it organizes all of this into a story that is complete with characters, setting, time, and plot—the very components of story itself. Dan McAdams notes, "Life stories are based on biographical facts, but they go considerably beyond the facts as people selectively appropriate aspects of their experience and imaginatively construe both past and future to construct stories that make sense to them and to their audiences, that vivify and integrate life and make it more or less meaningful" (McAdams, "The Psychology of Life Stories", 2001, p. 201).

Another way of putting this is to recognize that these stories organize, in their own unique constructions, the otherwise chaotic storeroom of life facts and dreams into a kind of coherency. Each person's Narrative Identity is an ordering of chaos into story-borne meaning.

Our stories change as we live. We can recall Erik Erickson's eight Psychosocial Stages first introduced in his acclaimed 1950 book *Childhood and Society*. The stages of life, according to Erikson, are periods of one's lifetime when major issues of identity are resolved.

Erikson's Psychosocial Stages

Stage	Basic Conflict	Important Events	Outcome
Infancy (birth to 18 months)	Trust vs. Mistrust	Feeding	Children develop a sense of trust when caregivers provide reliability, care, and affection. A lack of this will lead to mistrust.
Early Childhood (2 to 3 years)	Autonomy vs. Shame and Doubt	Toilet Training	Children need to develop a sense of personal control over physical skills and a sense of independence. Success leads to feelings of autonomy, failure results in feelings of shame and doubt.
Preschool (3 to 5 years)	Initiative vs. Guilt	Exploration	Children need to begin asserting control and power over the environment. Success in this stage leads to a sense of purpose. Children who try to exert too much power experience disapproval, resulting in a sense of guilt.
School Age (6 to 11 years)	Industry vs. Inferiority	School	Children need to cope with new social and academic demands. Success leads to a sense of competence, while failure results in feelings of inferiority.

Adolescence (12 to 18 years)	Identity vs. Role Confusion	Social Relationships	Teens need to develop a sense of self and personal identity. Success leads to an ability to stay true to yourself, while failure leads to role confusion and a weak sense of self.
Young Adulthood (19 to 40 years)	Intimacy vs. Isolation	Relationships	Young adults need to form intimate, loving relationships with other people. Success leads to strong relationships, while failure results in loneliness and isolation.
Middle Adulthood (40 to 65 years)	Generativity vs. Stagnation	Work and Parenthood	Adults need to create or nurture things that will outlast them, often by having children or creating a positive change that benefits other people. Success leads to feelings of usefulness and accomplishment, while failure results in shallow involvement in the world.
Maturity (65 to death)	Ego Integrity vs. Despair	Reflection on Life	Older adults need to look back on life and feel a sense of fulfillment. Success at this stage leads to feelings of wisdom, while failure results in regret, bitterness, and despair.

"Erikson's Psychosocial Stages Summary Chart."
https://www.verywell.com/eriksons-psychosocial-stages-summary-chart-2795742].

Narrative Identity psychologists say that our stories become self-conscious during the latter stages of adolescence but that, throughout the life span, how the basic developmental conflicts are resolved significantly affects the course of one's self-story.

Now, of course, we don't have to be psychologists to recognize that none of us adults understand ourselves today in the same way we did when we were adolescents. These major stages of psychosocial development are also laden with life events that, while they may be influenced by the stage we are in, significantly color the rest of our developing life stories.

Novelist and preacher Frederick Buechner never could comprehend his father's suicide which happened when Frederick was only ten. But in his 1983 autobiographical book, *Now and Then*, adult Frederick writes,

If I were called upon to state in a few words the essence of everything I was trying to say both as a novelist and as a preacher, it would be something like this: Listen to your life. See it for the fathomless mystery that it is. In the boredom and pain of it no less than in the excitement and gladness: touch, taste, smell your way to the holy and hidden heart of it because in the last analysis all moments are key moments, and life itself is grace (Buechner, 1983).

For Buechner, mystery—in both its awful and wondrous expressions—is a key part of his own Narrative Identity.

But even an important narrative life theme tells only a part of the story. Just as important is the way the theme is expressed. Remember, agency refers to a person's sense of having control of his or her life. In high agency, a person is an actor on the stage, causing things to happen. In low agency, a person experiences themselves as more of a spectator, watching his or her life be controlled by other people or things.

Communion refers to a person's drive to form friendships and relationships with others that are marked by appropriate intimacy, sharing, belonging, and affiliation. It describes those who accompany us on our life journey and the significance of their presence. In very high communion, however, the drive to be in close relationship could, in fact, lead that person to make self-harming decisions in order to develop or maintain one or more relationships. We call this co-dependency—a combination of low agency and too-high communion. In very low communion, a person is much less influenced by the need for acceptance and relationship with others but may then become immune to an awareness of hurting or overlooking others. In that short passage from Buechner, we learn nothing about agency or communion. How does he handle mystery? Has that theme connected him with other people or pulled him away? His two-volume spiritual biography (*The Sacred Journey* and *Now and Then*) reveals his struggles with both agency and communion. But always there was the belief that mystery is never a closed door. It always swings the door open to the future. Always there is the possibility for tough times to reveal growth in personal meaning.

McAdams proposes a simple coding process that researchers can use to identify the relative strengths of agency and communion in people (McAdams, "Coding Autobiographical Episodes for Themes of Agency and Communion", 2001 (r)). Even non-researchers can use some of the coding principles that he suggests. The questions can help us gain a clearer sense of the inner qualities of a disaster survivor we are working with. They can be handy as examples that help us focus on what we are hearing.

Examples of agency themes we listen for could include elements such as:

- A person strikes out on a new career path with the belief that he/she can be successful
- A person recognizes that he/she is not achieving full potential and decides to seek counseling to discover what is holding him/her back
- A person decides to begin a new and healthier lifestyle in order to be more effective at home or at work
- An actor seeks a coveted role in an upcoming play
- A man or woman begins training for a first 5k run
- A student sets getting on the Dean's List as this semester's goal

These are not specific things that one must do to exhibit high agency. They are instead examples of things that high agency may stir up in someone.

Similarly, there are indicators for high communion:

- A person highly values a new friendship
- Following a family death, a person immerses him/herself in family relationships
- Someone reaches out to neighbors who are ill

- A person loves getting together with friends for social occasions
- A parent feels truly connected with a child and works diligently to help that child be ready for "grown up" life
- A young person indicates that co-workers are an important part of work satisfaction

Again, none of these are in any way prescriptive. But they can be indications or pointers to the kinds of things we may hear that could clue us in to someone's high or low agency and communion. They are the kinds of things we can notice in Narrative Listening.

In the previous chapter we met Nikki, a woman who had been married to a man who repeatedly called her a "screw-up." This was so powerful that it became a key part of her own Narrative Identity. She did not cite other remarks she must have heard throughout her life about being good at this or that. Those positive remarks became buried beneath the thin and more powerful "screw-up" ones. With that key piece of her story in place, it was not a great leap for her to fear that the future would also be filled with screw-ups—including her attempts to recover from the flood and to assist her daughters in their own recovery. We would note that her sense of personal agency—or, if you will, personal potency—is likely quite low, and feeling confident about the future is difficult for her.

Redemption and Contamination

While agency and communion are two key themes in one's life story, they are affected by two others: redemption and contamination.

Redemption traces a self-story arc from a generally bad or negative state to a generally good or positive one. It includes experiences of and expectations for recovery, learning, and growth. A very low measure of redemption may indicate a sense of deep disillusionment in which one is vulnerable to succumbing to a sense of hopelessness, especially if tethered to low agency.

Contamination is much the opposite of redemption. It traces a self-story arc from a generally good or positive state to a generally bad or negative state. Contamination stories can reflect victimization, betrayal, loss, failure, and, again, disillusionment.

Both redemption and contamination themes are powerful influences about future expectations of meaning and well-being.

Listening to Nikki's story, we sense low agency with high contamination. It is as if she were saying, "I'm weak, and my weakness is going to make things worse." Her worry about her children, as we noted, may indicate a stronger theme of communion. But, is her communion theme expecting improvement (redemption) or deterioration (contamination) to happen? The theme of redemption seems nearly absent in the beginning of her conversation with Tracey. Nikki's story, when projected into the future, suggests that she expects to screw things up as she tries to help her daughters recover from the flood (agency with contamination) and a deep worry that she will take her daughters down with her (communion with contamination). Her future is a closed book.

In her conversation with Tracey, something begins to happen to Nikki. The creed-like affirmation that she can give birth to beautiful things begins to add redemptive notes to her story.

Sacred Story

Sometime in the early 1970s while I was still a young man in my mid-twenties, I was driving along in a familiar part of town. Actually, I was half driving and half looking for music on my car radio. I suddenly stopped. From the radio came something that I, as a product of the '60s, had never heard before. It sounded so familiar, yet I knew that I had never heard it. It wasn't rock; it was violins and cellos playing something beautiful. I stopped at that station, though, because it sounded so familiar. The broad sweep of its tones captivated me, and I kept listening and listening. I drove way out of my way just to avoid shutting the radio off. When the end of the piece came, I learned I had been listening to "Appalachian Spring" by

Aaron Copeland. The composer's name meant nothing to me. Later, I discovered that this wonderful music had been written all the way back in 1944 and was, of all things, an orchestral score for a ballet. Quite a different world than the Rolling Stones!

What was it about "Appalachian Spring" that felt so familiar? I had never listened to classical music, and even if I had, it certainly would not have been ballet music. Only later would I discover that Copeland was a master at writing "American" music—music that captured American tones, chords, and melodic metaphors. "Appalachian Spring" connected with me. So, many years later, I can explain it no better than saying I believe that it connected with something deep inside of me—that "American" thing. No experience that I am conscious of can explain this. It was just familiar. But why?

Somehow, buried deep within me was a familiarity with these tones, chords, and melodic metaphors. I can't explain how they got there, but that familiarity was certainly aroused that first time I heard "Appalachian Spring." All that was down there.

Earlier we took a quick look at Stephen Crites' suggestion that each of us bears both a (conscious) mundane story and a (deeply unconscious) sacred story. Narrative Identity is the stuff of mundane story. It is the conscious way we understand ourselves in all of our complexities. But Crites suggested that mundane story bubbles up from sacred story. Stored in sacred story are our experiences and familiarities, as well as the assumptions about ourselves and about life that these experiences form. It is at this level that we bear our understandings of how the world works and how we work within it. This is related to Janoff-Bulman's three basic life assumptions: the world is benevolent, the world is meaningful, and the self is worthy.

It is in the sacred story level of our existence that order gets formed out of the chaos of daily living. It is where story happens in its most pristine way. We cannot tolerate chaos. Story functions to bring order out of chaos. The stories we tell others about ourselves begin as sacred stories residing in our unconscious sacred turf. Let's turn our attention now to the role that sacred stories play in the story map of our lives.

Creating Our Story

Others have used different names to describe the same internal organization of life story. Dan McAdams prefers the name "personal myth." Here we refer not to the self-conscious stories we have created about ourselves but rather to a deeper and unconscious level of meaning-making.

Let's illustrate how these things begin. If, as an infant, we cry in distress because of the discomfort of a dirty diaper, and someone (a parent, most likely) comes, soothes us, and places us in a clean diaper, we have accumulated a story that, if put into words, would go something like this: "I received relief from my distress from someone who is loving and finds me worthy of being relieved, and this suggests that there is some kind of meaning and importance to my life." Of course, no infant is going to parse that experience in anything similar to that thought-string. But that is how we internalize it. Each time the soiled diaper gets changed after we cry, that story and those assumptions are reinforced.

Sadly, not all children would internalize this story. Abuse and neglect, illness and separation from sources of comfort, would paint that story with different colors. If those more negative things turn out to be the norm for this child, a very different unconscious personal myth or sacred story would grow in its power and would give birth, in turn, to a very different conscious schema. This is the same as saying that sacred story births mundane story and becomes attached to a schema.

Whatever terminology we may use, the same outcome is being described. We each develop our own unique expectation of how the world works and how we are able to work within it. Some of this sense is conscious, much of it is unconscious, and all of it is held in narrative form.

Nikki, we noted, disclosed in her conversation with Tracey a sense of low agency. That is, the "screw-up" schema bestowed on her by her former spouse led to low expectations that she would be able to successfully handle the major challenges that the flood had confronted her with. She was keenly conscious of her assumption that her future would be negatively impacted by her inability to do things well. But this doesn't add up, does it? She had performed well in getting herself and her daughters to the shelter but gives herself no credit for it, and she expects that she will not do well (that is, she will screw up) in the future. If we are listening closely, we will notice that there is a disconnect here. It doesn't add up.

What accounts for this disconnect? Why would it not be possible to simply point out to Nikki that she is a powerful and competent person and let that be the end of it? For that matter, why had her husband's labelling of her stuck in the first place? The list of life areas in which she was not a screw-up was quite long. But "screw-up" stuck. In other words, why can't the facts of her life change her assumptions? It doesn't add up.

Remember "Kadel's Law" mentioned earlier? It says, "When things don't add up, you are treading on sacred turf." Kadel's Law signals that something else is missing and may lie hidden in Nikki's sacred story.

For sure, if we were working with Nikki, we'd be aware that there is so much about her that we don't and cannot know. But, if we could open and read Nikki's sacred story, we would understand why it stuck and became a schema. We remind ourselves that a lifetime of experiences has preceded our first meeting with her. What we learn in our short time with her is important, but so much else has happened before. Nikki's life has had some powerful events and challenges that we will never know. Since we cannot know this part of Nikki's life, we surely could not use it in our work. But knowing that *something* is in that sacred story will keep our ears properly tuned to what she does share. In other words, story ears hear what is missing, as well as what is said. Much goes on beneath the surface of anyone we will work with. So, here is what we didn't hear but can at least notice in its absence.

What Tracey Didn't Know

As a young child, Nikki's parents had experienced marital problems that led to their eventual divorce. Prior to the divorce, like so many children in troubled homes, she had sought to bring harmony into her childhood home by working quite hard to diffuse tense situations. She used cuteness; she drew wonderful pictures to give to each parent; she tried anything and everything. But what stopped her parents fighting with each other was when she became a problem herself. When she misbehaved, they would stop yelling at each other and begin yelling at her. She succeeded in her quest to get her parents to stop fighting by becoming a screw-up. It was painful, but it worked. She discovered high agency (perceived cessation of parental problems) in the guise of low agency (screwing up). It was a redemptive hope all wrapped in the thinnest of stories.

She once told a school counselor a fairy tale about a witch who had cast an evil spell on the king and queen and turned their words to each other into boiling water, burning the other. In the tale, the young princess would get in between the king and queen when this happened and let the boiling water fall all over her. The king and queen fell in love with each other again because they no longer hurt each other. But the princess was left with burns all over her. In the fairy tale, she had perfectly described not only her plight but also her solution to it. This was her thin story solution.

When her real parents finally did separate and divorce, though, her unconscious strategy went into overdrive. But it failed. She screwed up. It didn't succeed. No amount of boiling water would help. Being a screw-up had morphed from a strategy into a schema. Buried deep within her sacred story was the complicated plot that she was a "screw-up at even screwing up." And isn't it common that so many persons like Nikki find mates who confirm the very qualities in them that they fear the most.

In our brief (and possibly only) conversation with Nikki, we would never hear this sacred story. At this moment, we just need to allow ourselves to be alerted to the fact that there *is* one, and it may hold the key to making things add up. This assists in avoiding pathologizing survivors. It helps remind us that the present disaster circumstance is experienced by Nikki within a lifetime of context. We won't help Nikki very much if we approach her as if she had just appeared on this planet and the disaster were the only experience she had ever had. And it certainly won't help Nikki if we hear her story as one laden with mental illness. If Nikki were later to follow up with a therapist, this life-theme would likely come out, but as DSCs, it is enough for us to be aware that some kind of story lay hidden there. This awareness may help guide us away from directly confronting Nikki's tight grip on being a screw-up. Such a direct confrontation to her sacred story and the schema it built would likely only draw forth from Nikki a strong resistance.

Developing a Story Map

During her conversation with Nikki, Tracey was constructing a map in her head. It was a map that contained Tracey's impressions and may very well be useful in her conversation. At first Tracey constructed this map in her mind but later discretely transferred it to paper.

If I wish to drive someplace that is new to me, I'll use a map. Okay, these days, I'm more likely to use the GPS system on my smart phone. But that system is built upon a map because a map shows the way from point A to point B. The map saves me from driving west when I should be driving east.

A story map does the same thing. It uses information from the stories we hear from disaster survivors and indicates a direction to go. But maps do another thing we may not think about. A map shows us a myriad of ways *not* to go. While driving, we don't need to be aware of the ways not to go. But in spiritual care, it is vital to be aware of them.

Things that we want to listen for and map are:

- Agency
- Communion

- Thick or thin story
- Redemption
- Contamination

Together, our impressions of these things begin to act as a map for us to follow. Just as importantly, they disclose ways we want to avoid going. Perhaps these maps are simply themes that we can keep track of in our heads. But we may find it helpful to construct a quick and easy visual map.

From her little bit of conversation, Tracey had what she needed to pull together a useful impression of Nikki and her story. She was given that map. The story map that Nikki gave to Tracey contained a great deal of information that can guide Tracey's care for her. Listening for agency, communion, redemption and contamination, and thick and thin story are the grids on that story map.

On her notepad, Tracey drew this very simple little diagram – a story map – to help her remember the narratives she had heard.

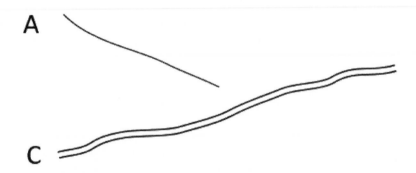

This simple little map began with Tracey's assessment of Nikki's sense of agency (A). Notice that it is a single line, which indicates "thin story", and that it is oriented downward, indicating contamination. It is a relatively short line, indicating that the sense of agency is not strong.

Below that is the line suggesting communion (C). It is a double line indicating a somewhat thicker story. Note also that it is an ascending line, which indicates redemption. The "C" line is a bit longer, indicating Tracey's perception that Nikki's sense of communion is somewhat stronger. Nikki's story contained many worries about her ability to take good care of her daughters as time moves forward, but Tracey also felt that, buried beneath her worries, was a determination to do whatever she needed to for them. These two little lines are all that Tracey needed to give herself a visual representation of Nikki's Narrative Identity – at least at this one particularly stressful point in time. As we look at this story map from the beginning of Nikki's conversation with Tracey, how would we write Nikki's creedal statement at that point? Remember, creedal statements describe beliefs. A creedal statement perceived at the beginning of a conversation may indicate a more useful creedal statement desired at the end. We have the beginning point on our map, and we have the end point. Tracey effectively used these two creedal statements to gain a sense of how to navigate that journey.

Try This

The beauty of the story map is that everything in it was gathered without prying from Nikki the actual account of her ordeal with the flood and thus avoided the risk of re-traumatizing her.

Remember Susan, the young mother described earlier who lost her husband in a tornado. Here, again, is an abridged version of how we described her:

> *A tornado stormed through Susan's little hometown. It wreaked massive destruction. Susan's husband was killed when their children began to cry for their beloved family dog Bootsy. Though he knew better, her husband still rushed out of their basement to try to rescue the dog. He and Bootsy didn't make it back. And, to layer tragedy upon tragedy, Susan's house was destroyed by the savage wind. She and her two little children somehow survived. But practically nothing was left of the rest of her life. It all lay in ruins amidst the rubble of their house. "How can this be?" she cried out. "Why?"*

She tried to make sense of her tragedy. She had tried to live a good life, so how could this happen? Nothing added up. She knew perfectly well that tornadoes are unpredictable and that her husband had made a bad choice, but that didn't answer why the storm had singled her and her family out. She described feeling a painful hole in her soul.

In the days following the tornado, Susan sought some kind of "something" that would make things add up. She remembered the argument she had had with her husband only hours before the tornado and how she had angrily yelled at him about looking for the dog. Was this her punishment for becoming so angry? She recalled one failure after another after another in her life until the sheer bulk of her failings began to add up to the scale of this punishment. She had been a flawed person, after all. Now she was flawed, widowed, and homeless.

Susan had trouble accepting assistance because something inside her kept telling her she didn't deserve it. This, connected with her grieving, sent her into emotional and physical isolation. As the days wore on, she became harder and harder on her children, and, if she had been able to put it into words, she would have said that she wanted to train them not to be as flawed as she was, not to experience the loss she had. Of course, it had the opposite effect on her children.

Something in her kept telling her that none of this was rational. Yet that voice had the lesser volume. Deep inside she harbored the belief, "I am flawed, and this causes suffering."

Try this. Put your imagination into gear. Imagine that you are with Susan a week or so after the tornado. She and her daughters remain in a shelter, and she has no idea where they will go. Based on the description above, make up a conversation between yourself and Susan that will account for the details in the description. Be sure to include not only the words that are spoken but also your observations of Susan's affect, as well as your intuitive sensing of the words not spoken.

Once you've written or at least imagined that conversation, draw a story map of it. Remember to include the agency (A) and communion (C) lines. How long should each be? Are those lines moving in a redemption arc or a contamination arc? Does each line reflect a thin or thick story? How would you phrase Susan's creedal statement at the beginning of the conversation? How would you phrase the creedal statement you would like to guide Susan into discovering and affirming?

Where are the hints of a sacred story buried between the lines of dialogue? How were those things phrased? Were there any creedal elements in the conversation explicitly spoken, and, if so, how were those phrased?

This, of course, is a purely imaginative exercise. There is no right or wrong way to do it. But hopefully it can help firm up the process of Narrative Listening. Narrative Listening reads between the lines and the lines themselves. It makes use of story-sensitive ears. Simply creating this imaginative dialogue may help bring that into focus. Pay attention to the difference between things that Susan says and things that you hear between the lines with your story ears.

Then, once you have created the dialogue, reflect on the experience of turning this description into the dialogue of your conversation with Susan. Did you find it easy or difficult to construct a story map from it? What was easier than you expected? What was more difficult? Was it difficult to discern the beginning creedal statement? Was it difficult to imagine and put that creedal statement into words?

It is important to note, once again, that the "sense" that emerged from your story map is just that—a sense of what is going on with Susan. This sense is very fluid and will likely change even during the course of your talk. Sense, in this case, is an intuitive thing, and that makes it quite different from data, which is evidence-based.

Finally, evaluate the dialogue you wrote. Did it keep the book of Susan's life open for her, or did it slam shut? Did you find it difficult to help keep the book open? If so, what made it difficult?

Summary

As we listen to the stories of disaster survivors, we can listen for key items that help define the state of the person we are talking with. We can listen for agency, which describes that person's sense of potency and individuality. We can also listen for communion which, describes a person's connections to others or their yearning for them. In addition, we can hear whether the person's story seems to be on a positive (redemptive) arc or on a negative (contaminated) one. These, together with the pointers picked up from listening for thick or thin "tellings," can guide us in developing conversational patterns that keep the book open. These maps may provide useful assistance in recognizing and working with creedal statements.

Preview

How do professed religious beliefs assist and/or hinder a person's ability to keep their book open to hope? As Disaster Spiritual Care responders, we will regularly work with people who are involved in a religion. Yet religions can vary greatly in the details of their belief systems and even more greatly in their practice. And what of those who have a religious identity but are not actually involved in it?

7

Religion and Dissonance

When Things Don't Add Up

I hear and I forget.
I see and I remember.
I do and I understand.

– Confucius

"On Friday noon, July the twentieth, 1714, the finest bridge in all Peru broke and precipitated five travelers into the gulf below." So begins Thornton Wilder's 1927 Pulitzer Prize winning novel *The Bridge of San Luis Rey*. The demise of the bridge and the deaths of the five unrelated travelers was witnessed by Brother Juniper. Wilder's novel explores the universal mystery about the nature of life and disaster. Brother Juniper is captured by the question "Why did this happen to *those* five?" Brother Juniper wonders, "Either we live by accident and die by accident, or we live by plan and die by plan." In the book, Juniper earnestly seeks the specific and unique reasons that the bridge collapse claimed these five particular lives. "Why did this happen to *those* five?"

It might seem that the work of a Disaster Spiritual Care responder should be a bit more simple when working with a person who identifies himself or herself as a member of a particular religion. We are, after all, working from the same set of assumptions about there being a God. But not so fast. Religion is a strength for so many people, but it may also be a source of confusion or even contradiction for the religious person experiencing trauma.

Earlier we considered Ronnie Janoff-Bulman's belief that there are three basic concepts that reside at the very heart of our assumptive worlds. So foundational are these assumptions that they infuse themselves into the ways we live our lives and understand

87

ourselves. They are that 1) the world/life is benevolent, 2) the world/life is meaningful, and 3) I am worthy.

But what happens to religious people when the world turns on them with terrible suffering or when life itself becomes unpredictable and chaotic? What happens to religious people when they lose much or all of what they have worked so hard to have?

It is no accident that the fate of one named Job has occupied an important place in three of the world's major religions—Christianity, Judaism, and Islam. Job's story traces undeserved sufferings that occur to him one after another. Is this God's doing? If so, why is God doing this? If not, is there a God at all? Even in religions that recognize many gods or that focus on one's unity/disunity with the natural world, undeserved suffering has claimed important roles. From the beginnings of recorded history, religions have wrestled with suffering. The universal question of undeserved suffering continues to perplex both religious and non-religious persons. Janoff-Bulman's three basic assumptions are framed within the context of psychology, but they literally throb also at the heart of spirituality.

What has gone before in this book has largely addressed Disaster Spiritual Care. But when we begin to think deeply about human suffering, all forms of disaster response are colored in one degree or another by the mystery of it. No one can escape the "why" of suffering. And if the psychological aspects of suffering were to be boiled off, profound spiritual ones will remain. Sometimes these profound religious ones can even add to the suffering.

We live in a time when causes are compulsively sought to explain consequences. It is the daily fare of politics when every negative national or local problem must be assigned a cause and blamed on an opponent. In sports, the cause and guilty party for every loss must be identified. Misfortune seeks causes, and tragedies must be connected to guilt. Someone or something must be the cause of everything that happens. The ancient Greeks infused into Western civilization the primacy of cause-and-effect. Our present scientific and technological age has raised this to new heights. In earlier times, mystery was a category that many things were assigned to. In our day, mystery is not its own category but may actually be experienced as a glove-slap signaling a challenge to solve.

Brother Juniper, wondering about the victims of the San Luis Rey bridge, could bring it down to only one fundamental issue. Either God is the cause of all things—good and bad—or everything is accidental and thereby constructed of chaos. If it is number one, why do bad things happen? If number two, why believe in God? The narratives that can emerge from either are quite limited. 1) God is punishing me or testing me. Or, 2) if accidental, then from where comes the possibility of hope? If 1), what do I do? If 2), why should I do anything?

Suffering is a universal dimension of the human condition. As we work with those who have experienced a disaster, we stand a 100 percent chance of working with those who are suffering in some degree and for one reason or another. As quoted earlier, but worth repeating, Dan McAdams noted,

> As William James (1902/1958) noted in *The Varieties of Religious Experience*, all the world's great religions begin with the problem of human suffering. Suffering originates in human flaws or frailties of some sort, or in the very nature of human existence. Thus, Christians and Jews speak of original sin whereas Buddhists ascribe suffering to dukkha, which denotes universal human conflict and sorrow. Each religious tradition suggests what human beings need to do or experience in order to be delivered from suffering to a positive state (McAdams & Jones, "Making Meaning in the Wake of Trauma: Resilience and Redemption", 2016).

The link between human suffering and religion is old, bold, and strong.

It behooves us, then, as care-givers within a world that is experienced through both assumptive expectations and cause-and-effect beliefs to explore more deeply how these things interact and, especially, how that interaction impacts the religious experience of those who are suffering. And, it is necessary for us to recognize that assumptive expectations and religious beliefs may often be in conflict.

Core Spiritual Assumptions: Benevolence

Let's begin to unpack this interaction by first asking if there are a set of religious assumptions that parallel Janoff-Bulman's psychological ones.

If the first psychological assumption is "The world is benevolent," can the spiritual parallel be "God is benevolent"?

I would suggest that there is a strong *spiritual* parallel but not so much a *religious* parallel. Let's look at the idea of God's benevolence within certain religious systems.

Jewish. At its heart, Judaism understands God as perfectly just and, at the same time, perfectly merciful. These two attributes are held in a mysterious tension. God is perfect, and perfection suggests justice. One receives what one deserves. Yet God is also understood to prefer mercy and encourages believers to live according to the Law in order that this mercy may be applied to them. Forgiving failures to live this way is in God's perfect nature, and in forgiveness, God's mercy is perfectly offered to those who seek it.

Christian. Growing from Judaism, Christianity shares the view of God as perfectly just. But the teachings of Jesus focus on God's determined benevolent desire and actions to restore humanity to the fullness of God's image. This is a restoration that humanity could not achieve on its own but was granted to believers through the crucifixion and resurrection of Jesus. Jesus is understood in much Christian theology as the one who experienced the just punishment of a fallen humanity resulting in his death. With this atoning death, believers are mercifully restored to a perfect relationship with God. This relationship is experienced "dimly" (or incompletely) during this life but fully in the resurrection of the believer.

Islam. Allah's benevolence is understood as being a reward for an earthly life lived in accordance with the teachings of the Prophet Muhammad and in good works towards others. Those who truly repent of falling short of these precepts are welcomed into heaven.

Eastern Religions. In Hinduism and Buddhism, gods or life forces can help humans only if they deserve it or are in harmony with the god or life force. Such deserving comes through the efforts of the believer. Grace plays a minor role.

Native American. Contemporary North American indigenous spiritual practices are enormously varied. The effects of European colonization upon the Native American populations were profound. Today's practices don't fit common Western "religious" categories. The many native peoples of North America had widely divergent spiritualties. Running through them in one sense or another, though, is a theme of oneness with others and with the created order. One cannot easily equate "God is benevolent" with any particular Western spiritual practice or belief. Yet, at the same time, benevolence is the understood nature of all that exists. Spiritual benevolence is simultaneously nowhere (in a particular sense) and everywhere (in a general sense).

The difficulty with understanding divine benevolence is, in a religious sense, rooted in the fact that benevolence is more understood in terms of human characteristics than in general spiritual ones.

Core Spiritual Assumptions: Meaning

What does exist, however, in religions is the assumption that there is some meaning to life and existence, though that meaning will differ greatly from one religious expression to another in both centrality and intensity. Thus, Janoff-Bulman's second assumption (The world/life is meaningful) can, with a bit of squeezing square pegs into round holes, more easily be translated into these spiritual terms: God (however understood) provides meaning.

The very fact that persons of all religions may face heavenward and cry, "Why?" suggests that whether that cry is rooted in a religious doctrine or not, meaning is, in one way or another, embodied into each. It is a spiritual thing.

Core Spiritual Assumptions: Worthiness

As a religious principle, worthiness is quite hit-or-miss across major religious expressions. Some would seem to teach that all persons are worthy but that this worthiness is something that must be sought, recovered, earned, or at least accepted. Other religions teach that worthiness cannot be recovered or earned, only be received as a gift. Yet, from a psychological standpoint, studies show that most people believe that the self (I am) is worthy.

Where Does This Leave Us?

Here is where all of this comes together. Psychologically, the vast majority of people do acknowledge benevolence, meaning and worthiness, as principles of their lives. Does this suggest that for many, there is a chicken-or-egg dilemma? Does religion color and inform core assumptions, or do core assumptions color and inform religion? That is meat for other disciplines to chew on.

As a spiritual care provider, what is important is to keep in mind that there is a kind of muddiness about all of this for many people. But it is an important muddiness. For instance, just because someone self-identifies as Christian does not mean that he or she believes (in their own personal case) that worthiness is a gift from God. One may believe that God bestows worthiness and at the same time feel themselves to be unworthy. With the broad expanse of Christian expressions, beliefs about God's benevolence, meaning-giving, and worthiness-bestowing cover a very wide expanse of interpretation. The same wide expanses exist within the other great religions as well. A valuable resource to learn basics of religious expressions and practices in the United States is the *Religious Literacy Primer* and its companion volume *Field Guide,* which were published in 2014 by the National Disaster Interfaiths Network (NDIN) and the University of Southern California Center for Religion and Civic Culture. It is available for free download from the NDIN website at http://www.ndin.org/ndin_resources/FieldGuideSet.php.

What should we take from this? First, it is important for us to have at least basic understandings of the various religious expressions that we are likely to encounter while on a deployment. Knowing, acting, and speaking within survivors' belief systems, as well as their rules and customs, are essential aspects of serving and honoring them. If we are unfamiliar with their religion and customs, we can just ask them. We honor them by asking. The opposite may be true if we assume or guess. We accompany them—if but for a short while—on a difficult and painful journey. Our accepting presence may be more meaningful than the words we speak.

But there is considerably more. Being with them comfortably and respectfully on this journey opens the door for them to trust us with their stories. It is how we enflesh the presence of God for them.

It is important to remain aware that disaster survivors are human beings full of the difficulties, challenges, complexities, and joys of living life. This affects even the most devoutly religious people. In deep ways, we share this profound similarity with those we serve. But still, these similar people will be full of their own unique contradictions and accommodations that they have made to the world, and it is likely that none of them will mirror any stereotypes of the cultures and religions they embrace.

I, for instance, am a member of the clergy of the Southeastern Pennsylvania Synod of the Evangelical Lutheran Church in America (ELCA), which is a mainline denomination of American Christianity. That is six levels of uniqueness to my religious identity: 1) *clergy* within 2) a particular *judicatory* (administrative level) of the denomination called the 3) *Evangelical Lutheran Church in America* which is a 4) *mainline* "type" of 5) *American* 6) *Christianity.* At each level, I can identify distinctions in my religious identity. I have much in common with all Christians, but not everything. But these distinctions are levels of uniqueness. And, even if someone is clergy in the ELCA, we may very well have unique approaches to understanding, say, the grace of God. And my life has been different than that of any other ELCA clergy, thus introducing yet another level of uniqueness of my religious experience and identity. Even if I were a responder to a disaster that affected only ELCA clergy, I would still need to remain aware that those I am there to serve will, in some important ways, be different from me.

As the variety of religious identities becomes richer, the complexity of actual religious beliefs will be impossible to chart. This indicates that our approach to these persons—even if they all seem to be of similar religious backgrounds—must be mitigated by the vast complexity of life-influenced beliefs. To be useful, we must be sensitive to and aware of these complex similarities and differences.

Even if survivors are all followers of a particular religious expression, it is a following that very likely has within it much that they have also fashioned, invented, or assumed. If they share that they have no religious connection, they may still have a deep and important spiritual core—even if they deny it.

The implications of these observations are important even if they seem to be common sense.

The Referral Rainbow

On one hand, persons who express particular religious questions must always (with their permission, of course) be referred to representatives of the religious expression they embrace. If Christian, the referral goes to a Christian expression. If Jewish, the referral goes to a Jewish expression. And so on.

But within each of those expressions, there will be a wide variety of teachings, views, and practices. With regard to Janoff-Bulman's core expectations of benevolence, meaning and worthiness, even the broad category called conservative Christianity, for instance, may include a vast array of interpretations all under the banner of Christianity. When that broadens out to include "mainline" and other expressions, the array of interpretations broadens into a mind-boggling number of colors.

So, if persons with whom we are working identify as Christian, it is still important to try to learn more before a referral is made. Referring a self-identified mainline Christian to a conservative expression of Christianity can, for instance, result in a disquieting dissonance. Our work attempts to assist these persons with experiencing comfort and this disquieting dissonance may only heighten the stress.

And this is just within Christianity. This rainbow of religious beliefs exists within each major religion. For example, Muslim believers range from those who understand the Prophet's teachings to focus primarily on peace and service to the poor to those who understand the Prophet's teachings to be primarily about justice and purity of doctrine. It is extraordinarily simplistic to understand all Muslim persons to have similar world views and core expectations.

Referrals within any religious expression should, to the best of our ability, be to those who represent that believer's place within the rainbow of beliefs within any given religion.

And there remains one additional level of complexity. Even among a group of persons who share an identical religious identity, there may be a vast array of "actual" beliefs. For instance, one's religion may express belief in a forgiving God, but that person may actually, on the inside, believe even more firmly in a God who is to be feared if one sins.

The Paralipsis Principle

Paralipsis is an infrequently used word that names a frequently used technique. It names a rhetorical device in which a speaker brings up a subject either by denying it or denying that it should be brought up. It comes from an ancient Greek term *paraleipein*, which means "to omit or leave something on the side." Paralipsis is frequently used in politics when a politician may say something like, "I'm not going to mention my opponent's ethical failings." The obvious intent of paralipsis in politics to raise something without raising something—to leave it on the side.

But paralipsis is also a great tool for DSC responders to be aware of. Sometimes things are left on the side because they are simply too loaded to say out loud. For instance, someone may feel anger at God for the suffering he or she is experiencing but cannot say it out loud. There may be religious taboos or fears to speak certain things. Sometimes the taboos are cultural. One may be concerned that expressing anger at God will elicit another's judgment or even abandonment.

Many years ago Charles Finn penned a poem, *Please Hear What I'm Not Saying,* that says this all so well:

> Don't be fooled by me.
>
> Don't be fooled by the face I wear
>
> for I wear a mask, a thousand masks,
>
> masks that I'm afraid to take off,
>
> and none of them is me.
>
> Pretending is an art that's second nature with me,
>
> but don't be fooled,
>
> for God's sake don't be fooled.
>
> I give you the impression that I'm secure,
>
> that all is sunny and unruffled with me, within as well as without,
>
> that confidence is my name and coolness my game,
>
> that the water's calm and I'm in command
>
> and that I need no one,
>
> but don't believe me.

My surface may seem smooth but my surface is my mask,

ever-varying and ever-concealing.

Beneath lies no complacence.

Beneath lies confusion, and fear, and aloneness.

But I hide this. I don't want anybody to know it.

I panic at the thought of my weakness exposed.

That's why I frantically create a mask to hide behind,

a nonchalant sophisticated facade,

to help me pretend,

to shield me from the glance that knows.

But such a glance is precisely my salvation, my only hope,

and I know it.

That is, if it's followed by acceptance,

if it's followed by love.

It's the only thing that can liberate me from myself,

from my own self-built prison walls,

from the barriers I so painstakingly erect.

It's the only thing that will assure me

of what I can't assure myself,

that I'm really worth something.

But I don't tell you this. I don't dare to, I'm afraid to.

I'm afraid your glance will not be followed by acceptance,

will not be followed by love.

I'm afraid you'll think less of me,

that you'll laugh, and your laugh would kill me.

I'm afraid that deep-down I'm nothing

and that you will see this and reject me.

So I play my game, my desperate pretending game,

with a facade of assurance without

and a trembling child within.

So begins the glittering but empty parade of masks,

and my life becomes a front.

I idly chatter to you in the suave tones of surface talk.

I tell you everything that's really nothing,

and nothing of what's everything,

of what's crying within me.

So when I'm going through my routine

do not be fooled by what I'm saying.

Please listen carefully and try to hear what I'm not saying,

what I'd like to be able to say,

what for survival I need to say,

but what I can't say.

I don't like hiding.

I don't like playing superficial phony games.

I want to stop playing them.

I want to be genuine and spontaneous and me

but you've got to help me.

You've got to hold out your hand

even when that's the last thing I seem to want.

Only you can wipe away from my eyes

the blank stare of the breathing dead.

Only you can call me into aliveness.

Each time you're kind, and gentle, and encouraging,

each time you try to understand because you really care,

my heart begins to grow wings—

very small wings,

very feeble wings,

but wings!

With your power to touch me into feeling

you can breathe life into me.

I want you to know that.

I want you to know how important you are to me,

how you can be a creator—an honest-to-God creator—

of the person that is me

if you choose to.

You alone can break down the wall behind which I tremble,

you alone can remove my mask,

you alone can release me from my shadow-world of panic,

from my lonely prison,

if you choose to.

Please choose to.

Do not pass me by.

It will not be easy for you.

A long conviction of worthlessness builds strong walls.

The nearer you approach to me the blinder I may strike back.

It's irrational, but despite what the books say about man

often I am irrational.

I fight against the very thing I cry out for.

But I am told that love is stronger than strong walls

and in this lies my hope.

Please try to beat down those walls

with firm hands but with gentle hands

for a child is very sensitive.

Who am I, you may wonder?

I am someone you know very well.

For I am every man you meet

and I am every woman you meet.

(Finn, Charles. "Please Hear What I'm Not Saying." Web. from website www.poetrybycharlescfinn.com. Used with permission)

"Please hear what I'm not saying" is a plea that says it all for many we will meet in our work. This is paralipsis writ large for the disaster survivor suffering from trauma. Hearing what that survivor cannot say may be the most extraordinary grace we can bring to them. And the paralipsis may very well be rooted in that survivor's belief that his or her feelings and religion are in conflict.

So how does one hear what a religious person is not saying? There is no recipe. As a responder we must rely on our gut. Here we can once again refer to what I called "Kadel's Law" — "When things don't add up, you are treading on sacred turf." When we sense a lack of congruence between the beliefs that are expressed and all those other "nonverbals" of communication, it may be a sign of paralipsis.

One of the most frequently cited studies of how messages are communicated comes from the work in the 1960s of Albert Mehrabian, currently Professor Emeritus of Psychology at UCLA. Those works suggest that 55 percent of communication is body language, 38 percent is the tone of voice, and 7 percent is the actual words spoken. These numbers have been significantly debated over the years, mostly on the basis of context. Context, the argument goes, can alter these numbers quite significantly (Thompson, "Is Nonverbal Communication a Numbers Game?", 2011).

Our purpose here is not to judge Mehrabian's numbers but to be reminded that, in the extraordinarily difficult circumstances religious survivors experience after a disaster, the words a survivor speaks may not be the full reality of what is going on within them. This may be particularly true if what the survivor believes religiously is different from what that survivor feels emotionally. We must rely on gut feelings.

What do we do?

It would be great if there were a solid recipe to follow when that dissonance is detected. But there isn't. But here are some approaches we may consider.

Make It Your Question

Remember that our goal is to help survivors keep the book open to hope. It is not a time to teach.

Suppose we are talking with a person who, reflecting a core religious belief, says, "I know this is God's plan" yet whose body and tone suggest otherwise. It is not a fruitful approach to respond, "Do you really believe that?" This will simply corner the survivor into defending a religious belief and very likely won't address the dissonance at all.

However, if we make the question our own, we may open a new pathway for the conversation. Consider responding, "I wonder if the things you've been through would cause me to wonder if God is fair." Now, the question belongs to us, and we are not yanking it out of that person. The book is open for any variety of paths for that person to follow. "Oh, I've never wondered that" may be the survivor's reply. This may signal that we incorrectly assessed the dissonance or that this person is not ready to talk about God's fairness. In either case, we are not putting words into that person's mouth, nor are we yanking anything out that isn't ready to come out.

The reverse situation may be followed the same way. Suppose that person says, "God is so unfair!" Again, this isn't a teachable moment, so we let go of that urge right away. We make the question our own. "I've had that same question sometimes, but I'm here because I believe that when the mystery clears up, I've always found God in the middle of it somewhere—and usually it comes as a total surprise to me. I wonder how that will work out for you?"

We have avoided closing the book on God's unfairness, but at the same time, we have not placed any kind of pressure upon that person to agree with us. In a positive application of paralipsis, we've said something without saying it. We've laid an idea out in the open and that idea can be examined any time the survivor is ready to do so.

Teach Me

Another way to explore a dissonance we pick up is to place the survivor in the more powerful position of teacher. "I know this is God's plan" may be followed by our request to have that person teach us more about that belief. Be ready, though, to hear a religious formulation. We may simply hear what that person has been taught to say. But we can make more "Teach me" requests. "Can you teach me more about how you understand God's plan for you?" With this response, we've opened the way for a person to connect religious teachings to the disaster experience itself.

The "teach me" approach allows the person to hold on to religious beliefs that are important but also offers that person the opportunity to hear his or her own answer. Some of us discover what we think or feel as we hear ourselves talk. This gets behind the religious teaching and leads into the personal experience. They may very well be in complete sync. Again, we do not accept the dissonance we picked up as a reality. We may have been wrong. The survivor may not be ready to explore the dissonance. Or the "Teach me" may disclose something completely different that is behind that dissonance.

Ask for a Report

One of the most common experiences that survivors have following a disaster is a rather rich and "thick" interaction with other survivors. The persons we are with may have had many conversations with other survivors before we first met them. It is quite likely that some of these conversations were about the very concerns we are addressing with them. For instance, a "God is so unfair!" conversation may have already been held with another. "What have you been hearing from others?" we could ask. Once again, we are placing that person in the more powerful position of being a reporter.

It may be less threatening to report someone else's worry about God's fairness than to report one's own. This may open avenues for us to explore. "Seems like everyone is wondering why God is so unfair" is the response. This is something we can easily affirm because the survivor is simply reporting. "How have you reacted to those conversations" might be our reply. Notice the use of the word "reacted" here. It is a far more helpful thing to ask for a reaction than a feeling. It allows one to describe feelings if ready but may, instead, open the opportunity to talk about physical reactions or even to describe events that happened during or after hearing that from someone else.

It has long been established that one of the most effective treatments for trauma is to be in a community of caring persons. To report on what others have said helps recall the communal experience of disaster and of disaster recovery. Usually (but not always), these early experiences with other survivors are supportive and compassionate. Even without suggesting that someone seek community healing, the very act of reporting the experience of others becomes a constructive paralipsis. We say something without saying it.

Reporting is also an opportunity for the person to tell how differently he or she is reacting than someone else is. By describing another's experience, that person is both connecting with the experience of others and differentiating her or his own experience.

And reporting has another possible benefit. Reporting the experience or conversations with others helps people measure and assimilate their own experience. In those conversations, our client may get the first opportunity to share their own experience and begin to find words for it. Being able to put words to a traumatic experience is a function of the cognitive brain and may relieve the amygdala of some or all of its responsibility to send alerts.

Summary

People who subscribe to and practice a particular religion may sometimes find themselves having feelings or questions that seem to contradict their religious understandings of God. When survivors wonder why suffering has come to their doorstep, their religious beliefs may seem to be in conflict with their emotional understandings of how the world works. Does God cause suffering? If so, why? If God does not cause suffering, is everything simply random? If that is true, another question may follow: does God even exist? Different religions may approach the answers to these questions in radically different ways. Even within a particular religious expression, one may find significantly different interpretations. This tells us that we must proceed into religious concerns very carefully and respectfully and that, if we decide to refer a survivor to a leader within a religion, we do that just as carefully.

In some cases, survivors earnestly want us to hear what they are unable or unwilling to say out loud. Paralipsis—saying something without saying it—may be the survivor's way of speaking the unspeakable. As Disaster Spiritual Care responders, we can make positive use of paralipsis to offer at least three different ways to speak the unspeakable: make it your question, ask the survivor to teach you about something, or ask for a report.

Preview

In recent years, there has been a marked increase in the number of North Americans who subscribe to no particular religion. How does one do Disaster Spiritual Care with persons who are not religious? In the next chapter, we will look at the rise of the "Nones" (as they are often called) and discover that, no matter why they are not religious, they may have a rich spirituality. How do we work with them?

8

"None" Does Not Mean Nothing

Caring for Those with No Religious Connection

"I believe in God, but not as one thing, not as an old man in the sky. I believe that what people call God is something in all of us. I believe that what Jesus and Mohammed and Buddha and all the rest said was right. It's just that the translations have gone wrong."

— John Lennon

Ed met thirty-five-year-old Eric in Eric's hospital room. Eric was hospitalized the day before when he experienced a rather marked episode of difficulty breathing while trying to clear a tree that had fallen onto his house during the hurricane. The house had significant damage to the upper level, but he, his wife, and their two young kids had decided that they could safely remain there. But now, here he was, tied to a heart monitor and with a breathing tube in his nose. His gratitude that he and his family had escaped injury from the storm was now eclipsed by his frustration at being in the hospital and unable to care for his family or their house.

Eric scanned Ed cautiously as he walked into the room and introduced himself.

"I don't need any spiritual care," Eric blurted. "I need to get out of here and take care of my house. Tree fell on it."

"Much damage?"

"You bet, but nothing we can't handle. Again, thank you for stopping, but, frankly, the last thing I need right now is God-talk. I hope you aren't offended."

"Not at all offended," answered Ed. "Sounds like you've been through it!"

"Lots of folks had it worse. At least my wife and kids are okay."

"Someone helping them while you are here?"

"Yeah, a neighbor is looking in on them. We've grown close to them over the past few years. We look out for each other. But I need to get out of here and take care of things. I'm okay."

"What happened that ended you up here in the hospital?"

"Had some shortness of breath while trying to get that tree off my house. Maria—that's my wife—got all worried and told me to get into the car, and she drove me here. Guess she did that out of love, but I was okay even before we got in the car. Got here and they decided to hook me up to this thing," he said, pointing to the heart monitor in his hospital gown pocket. "Anyway, thanks for stopping by, but like I said, God-talk is the last thing I am interested in right now."

"Frankly, Eric, if I were here away from my family at a time like this, I think I'd be plenty frustrated right now."

"Got that right."

"How might I be able to help? Would you like me to check in on your family?"

"Maria's not going to be interested in God-talk either."

"That's fine. But maybe there are some other ways I can help you all."

"Like what?"

"Well, for one thing, I can check to make sure they've got all the food and water they need and reassure them that you are okay. And I can help you connect with any other things you may need."

"Didn't you say you are a spiritual care guy? I figured you'd be going around praying with people. But if you'd like to check in on my family, that would be good."

"Sometimes meeting a basic need is the most spiritual thing I do."

"Hmm."

"You sound a little surprised."

"Oh, I gave up the idea of God a long time ago. It just doesn't make sense. I'm an engineer, and I know how stuff works. There aren't any miracles. Everything can be explained one way or another. And church people? Forgive me, but they are the worst—always trying to get people to think they are better than everybody else. I'm just staying way away from all that."

"Me too."

"But you said you were some kind of spiritual guy," Eric said, cocking an eyebrow.

"I am. But I'm here to let you know that there are people who care about what you and your family have been through and to see if there is any way I can help out."

"Hmm."

Ed had been making mental notes about his conversation with Eric. If he had sketched a story map on paper, it would have looked like this:

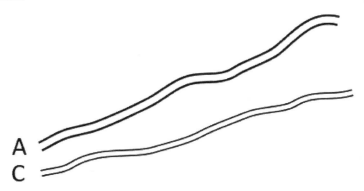

A
C

Ed heard Eric's sense of agency (A) in his confidence that he could take care of his family and that his house would eventually be fixed. Ed considered this a very strong (long line) expectation and that his telling of it seemed thick (line is double). Ed seemed quite sure that things would work out; thus, the line traces up.

He also sensed that Eric's communion (C) arc was strong, thick, and optimistic as well. Ed picked up on this by Eric's commitment to care for Maria and his daughters, as well as the relationship he described with his neighbors. In his mind, Ed framed Eric's creedal statement as "I believe I have the ability to lead my family through this temporary setback."

But there is another factor at work in this conversation, and it may give a DSC a bit of pause.

Eric is a "None"—one of a demographically growing part of the American population that claims no religious affiliation. That is, at least, where he would be counted by any of the many studies that seek to measure religion in American life. Thirty-five years ago he was born into a somewhat active Christian family, went to Sunday School, and worshipped with his family fairly regularly. But when Eric went off to college, he stopped attending church. If we had asked him back then if he believed in God, he would have said, "Sure." But as time passed, his connection to his religious faith diminished even more. After college, he married Maria, had two great kids, and became quite involved in his work. The "real world" for Eric was building a family and working hard.

Eric is a good man who lives his life according to values that he has embraced and holds himself to. His rejection of the idea of God actually fits into and is partially shaped by those very values. Integrity is the cornerstone for those values, and he rejects the idea of claiming a belief in God when he actually does not have that belief. His life is lived largely without reference to or consideration of the possibility of God. However, he does not use the term "atheist" to describe himself because, to him, that term suggests being "anti-God", and he does not consider himself as being "anti" anything. For Eric, the question of God is simply irrelevant in an age of science and high technology.

Had Eric asked Ed about God, Ed's faith story and witness might be amazingly powerful. But that is a door that Eric must open, not Ed.

How do spiritual care responders connect with people like Eric who do not consider themselves either religious or spiritual? This is an important question. Let's look at some numbers.

Who are the "Nones"?

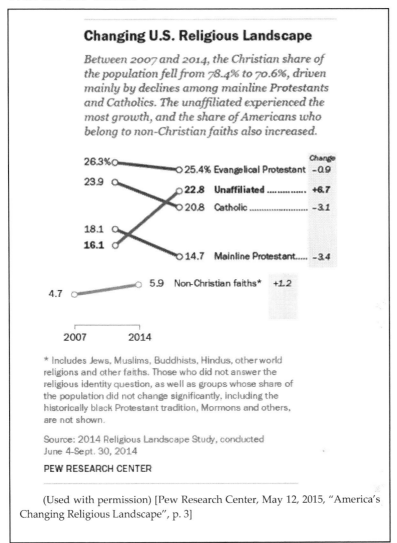

Changing U.S. Religious Landscape

Between 2007 and 2014, the Christian share of the population fell from 78.4% to 70.6%, driven mainly by declines among mainline Protestants and Catholics. The unaffiliated experienced the most growth, and the share of Americans who belong to non-Christian faiths also increased.

	Change
26.3% → 25.4% Evangelical Protestant	-0.9
23.9 → 22.8 Unaffiliated	+6.7
→ 20.8 Catholic	-3.1
18.1	
16.1 → 14.7 Mainline Protestant	-3.4
4.7 → 5.9 Non-Christian faiths*	+1.2

2007   2014

* Includes Jews, Muslims, Buddhists, Hindus, other world religions and other faiths. Those who did not answer the religious identity question, as well as groups whose share of the population did not change significantly, including the historically black Protestant tradition, Mormons and others, are not shown.

Source: 2014 Religious Landscape Study, conducted June 4-Sept. 30, 2014

PEW RESEARCH CENTER

(Used with permission) [Pew Research Center, May 12, 2015, "America's Changing Religious Landscape", p. 3]

The number of "Nones" has been on the rise in North American for many years particularly with those once who identified with the Christian and Jewish faiths. The Pew Research Center has traced religious affiliation for many years. A 2015 web posting [http://www.pewresearch.org/fact-tank/2015/08/27/10-facts-about-religion-in-america/] identified a number of key facts about religion in America.

Between 2007 and 2014, significant changes have happened within the broad Christian spectrum. Notice on the graph that Evangelical Protestants, Catholics, and mainline Protestants have all declined as a percentage of the American population. A modest increase was experienced in the grouping of persons practicing non-Christian faiths (including Jews, Muslims, Buddhists, Hindus, and others). But the largest increase came in the group of persons identified as "Unaffiliated." These would be the "Nones."

But "Nones" are a very diverse group. Some have never had a religious affiliation. The meanings of religious symbols, words, and texts are generally unknown to them. Other "Nones" are ones who, like Eric, once had an affiliation but no longer do. They may or may not have a sense of the meanings of religious fundamentals. And the complexity only thickens within that "once-but-no-longer" group. Some have just fallen away because of indifference to their earlier faith. Some have left the faith because they are suspicious of organizations in general. Yet others have left because they oppose practices (official or unofficial) of the faith in which they were raised. And, of course, some have left their childhood faith because they just don't believe it anymore.

Seventy-eight percent of today's "Nones" were raised in a faith "before shedding their religious identity in adulthood" (Lipka, 2016). In that same article, Michael Lipka organized into four broad categories the Pew study identified as causes of a lack of affiliation with American religion:

- They don't believe
- They dislike organized religion
- They are religiously unsure/undecided
- They are inactive believers

In a nation in which the majority of the population still claims a religious affiliation, we are still likely to encounter one in five survivors of a disaster who consider themselves unaffiliated with any religion. More than 20 percent of Americans are "Nones." That percentage is growing.

Within Judiasm, things are even more complex. We use the same term, Jewish, to describe the considerable range of religious beliefs and practices among Jewish people. We also use that same term to describe ones who might describe themselves as "cultural Jews." These are persons who do not practice the faith but remain connected through family, cultural ties, or their connection to the nation of Israel. The bellwether often cited is the rather rapid increase in the rate of Jewish people marrying partners from outside the faith. "The percentage of 'Jews of no religion' has grown with each successive generation, peaking with the millennials (those born after 1980), of whom 32 percent say they have no religion" (Goodstein, 2013).

By contrast, the third largest religious group in the U.S., Islam, is growing, and projections show it will continue to grow.

According to the Pew Research Center, "in North America, Muslims and followers of 'other religions' are the fastest-growing religious groups."

In the U.S. specifically, "the share of the population that belongs to other religions is projected to more than double...rising from 0.6 percent to 1.5 percent." Unlike the current global trend, where Christianity is projected to continue increasing, "Christians are projected to decline from 78 percent of the U.S. population in 2010 to 66 percent in 2050, while the unaffiliated are expected to rise from 16 percent to 26 percent."

Pew Research Center data also suggest that, barring cultural and ethnic Jews categorized as "unaffiliated" in their survey, "by the middle of the twenty-first century, the United States is likely to have more Muslims (2.1 percent of the population) than people who identify with the Jewish faith (1.4 percent)" (Morris, "Muslims Fastest Growing." http://www.cnsnews.com/blog/michael-morris/).

But these trends only tell part of the story. A more substantial part of this story is the question of how *important* is one's religion. This sense of importance is what we encounter with the persons we serve at a disaster site. Again, Pew's Religious Landscape Study in 2014 begins to answer that question.

Importance of Religion by Religious Group

Religious tradition	Very important	Somewhat important	Not too important	Not at all important	Don't know	Sample Size
Buddhist	33%	39%	15%	10%	2%	264
Catholic	58%	32%	8%	2%	< 1%	7,202
Evangelical Protestant	79%	17%	2%	1%	1%	8,593
Hindu	26%	53%	15%	6%	< 1%	199
Historically Black Protestant	85%	12%	1%	1%	< 1%	1,916
Jehovah's Witness	90%	8%	< 1%	< 1%	1%	245
Jewish	35%	36%	20%	9%	< 1%	847
Mainline Protestant	53%	34%	10%	2%	1%	6,083
Mormon	84%	12%	3%	1%	< 1%	664
Muslim	64%	24%	8%	2%	1%	237
Orthodox Christian	52%	33%	12%	3%	< 1%	186
Unaffiliated (religious "nones")	13%	21%	26%	39%	1%	7,556

("Importance-of-religion-in-ones-life." Pew Forum. 2016. Web, http://www.pewforum.org/religious-landscape-study/importance-of-religion-in-ones-life/)

So, we return to the question of this chapter: How do spiritual care responders connect with people who do not consider themselves religious or even spiritual?

Ed did it well. He kept his priorities firmly in mind. Ed faithfully followed Eric's lead. Our work is always focused on following the lead of those we work with. Notice that Ed was clear that he was in Eric's hospital room to offer assistance, not to convert him to any particular faith expression. When we keep this in mind, someone's objections to the idea of God, their anger at God, and even their indifference about God do not become points for debate or correction. They remain what they should be—issues that may affect a person's source of hope. Ed was there as God's enfleshed presence, not as God's agent.

Disaster is Not a Teachable Moment

Some responders belong to religious groups that firmly believe that witnessing to God and converting a survivor to a certain belief system is a core value of disaster response. That is wonderful in the right time and place. But let me say this rather bluntly: trauma victims are in a very different place following a disaster than they were in their pre-disaster lives. If I can make this particular distinction, trauma victims are not "teachable", but they are highly "susceptible." The traumatic state has one primary goal: survival. If one senses that survival is somehow more likely if he or she agrees to a helper's urgings, those urgings may be difficult, if not impossible, to resist.

This vulnerability is, I believe, a unique version of the Stockholm Syndrome. In 1973, several bank employees were held captive inside the Swedish bank for six days. When the assault was finally over, the world was shocked by the bank employees' expressions of sympathy and understanding of their captors. One quick and simple definition of the Stockholm Syndrome is that it is a captive's loyal response to his or her captor. But it is far more complicated than that. It is sometimes explained in terms of bonding and attachment theories, which describe one's instinctual response of partially merging "selfs" with another on whom one has become dependent for survival.

When someone has experienced the trauma of a disaster, he or she can become quite dependent upon those who arrive to help them. The greater the need, the deeper the dependence goes. If that traumatized person has become dependent upon a disaster spiritual care provider, there will be an almost irresistible urge to keep that responder near, which may include agreeing to whatever view of God the responder suggests. So these "conversions" are not conversions at all but actually expressions of abuse—no matter how unintentional. That sounds harsh, but this is so important that it needs to be stated this way. This also explains why the disaster survivors themselves must always lead the way into spiritual conversations.

We believe in a loving God who never abandons the weakened ones but strives to help make them whole again. This may sound like the very witness that this struggling person needs to hear. But if that witness is offered prematurely or inappropriately, the survivor may "convert" but later become extremely vulnerable to profound disappointment or despair if that recovery of well-being doesn't happen immediately or within a seemingly reasonable span of time. Instead of assisting someone to keep the book open to hope, this may slam it shut.

Progression and Regression

There is yet another dynamic that relates to our work with disaster survivors, especially with "Nones."

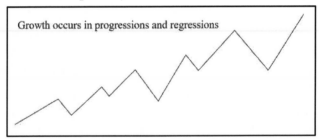

Growth occurs in progressions and regressions

It is a well-established fact that no growth happens on a straight upward line. It is actually a rather jagged line: progression, then regression, then more progression, then another regression. It goes on and on.

Years ago, when I left parish ministry to join a family therapy practice full time, there was a day when I was setting up my new office. I had a number of new bookshelves to assemble. I am somewhat handy at things like this, but that day I just couldn't get those shelves together. Everything I did went wrong, and nothing went together correctly. In the midst of my frustration, my new partner showed up, and I told her how I couldn't get those bloomin' shelves together. She laughed and asked me if I remembered anything I had learned about human development. "You're overwhelmed and are in a regression," she said. "Right now, you are a little kid trying to do a grown-up task."

She was absolutely right. When overwhelmed, we tend to regress to earlier and safer times in our lives. It helps us handle the anxiety of all the newness. Think of a toddler at the mall with her mother. Mom stops to talk with someone, and the toddler hangs on Mom's leg. After a bit, something catches the toddler's eye, and she heads for it. Suddenly the toddler realizes that Mom is out of reach. This big, new world of the mall is exciting, but it is also terrifying. Anxiety overcomes curiosity, and the toddler quickly returns to Mom and grabs hold of her leg again. This regression calms the little one's anxiety, but soon something else catches her eye, and she heads off to it. This time she makes it a step or two further from Mom before the anxiety overwhelms her and she dashes back. The toddler in the mall is a magnificent example of the pattern we all follow when thrust into a new and overwhelming situation.

If life has just been turned upside down by a disaster, one may experience a strong need to deal with the sudden anxiety. A regression to a safer and more sure time of life is in the offing!

Now, let's think about that "None." The religious demographic group called "Nones" now comprises the second largest religious group in the United States—second only to evangelical Christians. And recall that nearly 20 percent of Americans are now considered "Nones." Of that large number, 49 percent were raised in a religion but left that religion because of lack of belief (Lipka, 2016).

When "Nones" regress spiritually, they are likely to regress to childhood beliefs. But remember, this is because of their trauma-related anxiety. People of faith may be encouraged by what they hear. But we need to keep in mind that this is probably a trauma-caused regression. Again, our response is to follow them wherever they lead us, but we remain careful not to jump into the driver's seat ourselves.

Let's imagine a young mom named Allyson who, along with a number of others, had lost her home to a wildfire. When Allyson spoke about God to the DSC who was visiting with her, she shared that all this had caused her to think again about God, even though she had rejected the idea of God years earlier. Her DSC didn't shout "Alleluia!" about a re-conversion but simply and calmly asked about her childhood faith, its comforts, its encouragements, and its certainties. This experience may result in Allyson re-evaluating her adult religious views, but her DSC properly approaches this as a "keep the book open" conversation. For Allyson, hope may be born again from her memories of the religion she once was part of. Or it could be her emotional return to Mom's leg. Hope is the thing that keeps that book open. The reduction of anxiety that this return gives her could become an essential part of that hope. A childhood faith— the product of her well-deserved regression—will also have all the limits as well as wonderments of that earlier faith. Perhaps Allyson will be open to talking with a leader from her former faith to explore it as an adult. That may be the very thing that will end up sustaining her through the long ordeal of recovery. If the DSC encourages the childhood version, though, it may in fact be a "book closing" situation that will soon enough deliver deep disappointment when she attempts to apply it to grown-up challenges.

"None" Does Not Mean Nothing

Spirituality and faith are deep and vexing things all wrapped up in mystery. Had St. Teresa of Calcutta been surveyed by Pew in 2014, she almost certainly would have been termed a "None." In the newly publish book of her letters, there is one letter, written in 1956, that contains these sentences: "Such deep longing for God— and...repulsed—empty—no faith—no love —no zeal. (Saving) souls holds no attraction—Heaven means nothing—pray for me please that I keep smiling at Him in spite of everything." And then in 1959 she wrote, "If there be no God—there can be no soul—if there is no Soul then Jesus—You also are not true" (Mother Teresa & Kolodiejchuk (ed.), *Mother Teresa: Come Be My Light*, 2016).

No one, though, would suggest that Mother Teresa was a blank slate with regard to God. She saw and served unimaginable misery in Calcutta. There is little doubt in my own mind that she lived deep within the dark woods of secondary trauma. We'll look more deeply into secondary trauma in the next chapter. But such time had to have had a profound impact on her. Trauma does that—even to those who simply serve and serve simply.

Had we met this little wisp of a "None," we would not have written her off as an "unbeliever" and moved on to the next person. "Nones" are often deeply spiritual people. We would have recognized that she was not a person empty of faith but rather one who was full of disaster.

The "None" we meet in the shelter may be another St. Teresa.

Novelist Anne Lamott perhaps said it best when she observed "the opposite of faith is not doubt, but certainty."

Summary

One in five people we meet following a disaster are likely to have no religious affiliation. This growing group is referred to as the "Nones", but the label itself may be quite misleading. "None" does not mean nothing. They came to be religiously unaffiliated along many paths. But there is still great and powerful opportunity for Disaster Spiritual Care responders to assist them during this traumatic time in their lives. The key is to let them remain in the driver's seat. If they want to hear our ideas about God, they will ask. They are moments of raw need, and that need requires sensitive listening and helping. It requires that enfleshed presence of God.

Preview

Secondary trauma is an oft-neglected or unrecognized factor in the lives of those who experience disaster second-hand. Responders see and experience things that are so out of the ordinary that they often become overwhelmed in their own traumatic response.

How do we care for others who may be experiencing secondary trauma? And, just as important, how do we care for ourselves?

9

Secondary Trauma

The First Thing You Need to Account For

"In everything do to others as you would have them do to you."

— Matthew 7:12a (NRSV)

Corollary: Everything you do to others, you should do to yourself, too.

In the aftermath of 9-11, Gary and Lynne Jaeger responded to Ground Zero as counselors with the Disaster Chaplaincy Corps of The Chapel of the Four Chaplains. They were there to care for the chaplains and other responders. Several of those workers inquired what the "C4C" on their helmets and jackets meant and why they were there. They responded, "We're here so you don't have to be alone with this."

Their reply was perfectly simple and simply perfect. These responders were going through the hell of searching for victims and working horrible shifts doing so. "I'm here so you don't have to be alone with this" is a wonderful expression of enfleshed presence. No responder can function long or well if he or she feels all alone amid a myriad of others. This is a key pillar of Disaster Spiritual Care.

In her groundbreaking work on trauma, Judith Herman defines trauma this way: "Traumatic events are extraordinary, not because they occur rarely, but rather because they overwhelm the ordinary human adaptations to life" (Herman, 1992, p. 33).

But, in recent years, there has developed an understanding that trauma can also be experienced by those who are not directly impacted. The firefighter at Ground Zero may or may not have been there when the buildings came down. But the horror of that event could not possibly have left him unaffected. Many call this "secondary trauma." CISM International, an organization that offers Critical Incident Stress Management, uses a process for aiding first responders who have experienced primary or secondary trauma. On their website, they say:

> It has only been in the last 25 years that we have come to an understanding of how critical events affect human beings. The studies of traumatic impact began in earnest with the return of the Viet Nam veterans in the late 1960s and early 70s. However, historical records contain anecdotes of the problem since the sixth century B.C. Names such as shell shock, soldier's heart, combat stress, battle fatigue, stress breakdown, rape trauma, child abuse and battered wife syndromes have been given to the phenomenon. Since 9/11, we have come to realize how a whole nation can be traumatized by witnessing horrific events ("Critical Incident Stress Management" http://www.criticalincidentstress.com/traumatic_imp act).

Secondary trauma—sometimes also called compassion fatigue or even burnout—is commonly referred to as "the stress resulting from helping or wanting to help a traumatized or suffering person" (Figley, 1995, p. 7). Even those seemingly "removed" from the location of the actual event can experience it. Television, radio, and social media can arouse an overwhelming, but impossible to fulfill, urge to help those we see directly experiencing a terrible event. We need not be near the disaster to experience its trauma. We only have to be "overwhelmed" by it.

Secondary trauma is less often referred to but a very important focus for Disaster Spiritual Care responders. We need to be aware of it in ourselves and be on the lookout for it in those who respond alongside us. Secondary trauma is something that can haunt lives as much as primary trauma can, but, because those who experience it are less likely to recognize or less willing to admit to it, it frequently affects lives over long periods of time.

In You

Responders have chosen to assist others who have experienced a disaster. This is a necessary and vitally important calling. It may seem to run against every instinct in us, but there are times that we must "stand down"—both physically and emotionally. But this is very difficult. No one becomes a responder in order to sit on the sidelines while others bear the load of caring. But there are times that we must. If we don't, we may make things worse for ourselves and those we serve.

If we do not stand down when we need to, we may acquire self-destructive ways of coping with all that we are holding on the inside. No responder would tell a disaster victim to "get on with it" and ignore increasing signs of impairment. But that is just what many responders tell themselves.

My dad was always happy to show a business card he had received from his unit chaplain during World War II. In the overwhelm of infantry combat, I suspect that many soldiers had conversations with chaplains. This particular card, though, was given to him and others by the chaplain as something of an ice breaker. It had the chaplain's name and unit identification of one side. On the other in large bold letters it said, simply, "TS." At the bottom the initials were explained in small print: "Tough Shit." Dad was careful to explain that the chaplain wasn't sending him away but trying, in that army sort of way, to put things into perspective. The card meant enough to him that he kept it in a cigar box full of other "souvenirs" for the remainder of his life.

We wouldn't say TS to a disaster victim. We shouldn't say it to ourselves either.

Trauma calls out for us to try to handle or overcome a perceived threat. And we wouldn't be responders if handling a traumatic event were easy for human beings. But any of us may try to trick ourselves into believing that we are made of different—read, "stronger"—stuff and deny ourselves the very physical and emotional attention that we are trained to offer to others. This is how we give ourselves a TS card. Doing this can be equated to the proverbial road paved with good intentions and we all know where that road leads—a personal hell.

Those who have received training to be a responder have almost certainly learned about the importance of self-care and how to practice it ourselves. It is usually taught as one of the final subjects during basic training. After one or two intensive days of training, we may have glazed over when we got to this. I am not going to repeat the good stuff from earlier training. But self-care is vitally important to those we serve. We must make a similar commitment to do for ourselves what we know we need to do. Anything less, and we are giving ourselves a TS card and not only asking for trouble but displaying a vice that we probably don't want to have. We are bathing in the deceptive waters of *hubris*—pride. Those waters appear placid, but beneath the surface is a rip tide that can draw any of us out into very deep water.

One Trauma Behind?

A while back I approached a man at a reception center for persons who had been criminally cheated out of lots of money. As victims of crime, many who were there were experiencing the trauma of being cheated out of thousands of dollars. This man, though, was in good spirits and welcomed me with a big smile. But the very first words out of his mouth were "Hi! I was dead, but now I'm alive!" I thought maybe I had misheard him, and perhaps my face showed it. So, he repeated it. "I was dead, but now I'm alive!"

I began talking with him, and quite soon into the conversation he began telling me about an experience from his time as an Army medic in Vietnam. While encamped atop a high hill, a serious thunderstorm quickly came upon him and his platoon. In an instant, things went black. He awoke eighteen hours later. But everything was dark. Something kept him from moving. The "something" was all around him. He felt for and found his knife and cut a slit in the "something." He sat up and to his astonishment, he was in a morgue tent—one of many soldiers in body bags. Just then someone walked in, and the two men frightened each other. That's when he learned what had happened. He had apparently been struck by lightning. As he showed no signs of life, he was declared "killed in action." My new friend had been struck by lightning, declared dead, placed in a body bag, and laid in the morgue tent.

For this man, now approaching seventy years old, this had understandably become the most notable event in his life. I suspect that it was also the most traumatic event in his life. He told his story win thick detail and with eyes ablaze. Though he did, indeed, tell it as a past event, I was not at all certain that some part of him wasn't reliving it—for the several thousandth time.

When he had told me his story twice, he calmed down and began to quickly tell the story of why he was there at the reception center.

Those who have had training in therapy or counseling may have heard the saying, "We are always at least one grief behind." This saying is something of a reminder that, many times, when people experience a loss, they may end up not only grieving the present loss but also some past loss that hadn't been completely processed.

I would suggest that many disaster survivors and responders are also at least one trauma behind. Trauma and grief are closely related, and one is often, if not usually, a part of the other. When this is the case, big trauma can become an overwhelming and perhaps paralyzing trauma.

Sometimes, those we work with will clearly signal that the trauma of the present disaster is closely tied to earlier traumas. This was the case with my new friend. He openly and willingly told of the old trauma. But it also seemed that he had at least partially separated it out from other difficult times. There will be more about that separation in a moment.

But, more often, disaster survivors and responders simply experience old and present traumas in one big glob. We can be of significant service to these persons, even if our time with them is brief. While it is more art than science, we may develop a sense that the disaster experience they are describing just doesn't seem to account for the level of trauma they are displaying. No two people experience trauma in exactly the same way. But this "bigger than expected" trauma just might be a signal that there is more going on. By itself, it proves nothing, mind you. But it can be a very important signal.

If this person seems to need to talk about the trauma, the door may already be open for a simple observation. "I wonder if this experience has brought up memories of any earlier really tough times?" If he or she does, indeed, recall an earlier experience, something of significance may have just begun.

The present trauma is not likely to be easily attended to until it is mentally separated from former experiences. But that separation may provide the opening for identifying the trauma that belongs to the present circumstance as separate from the trauma of earlier circumstances. Each trauma needs to be recognized and honored.

If this person does identify an earlier trauma, it is important to let him or her lead the way regarding the depth and detail. Our work is to help this person keep the book open, not to slip into becoming a therapist. Honor all traumas that are identified—no matter how long ago they occurred. Observe how living with trauma is a difficult way to live. If appropriate, ask how they perceive God's presence in both the present trauma and any former ones. Perhaps a person may recall feeling divine help in the former one, and this may very well be just the awareness needed for the present circumstance.

Again, we remind ourselves that, no matter what other training we may have had, we are serving as a Disaster Spiritual Care responder, not as therapists. But the very act of separating one trauma from another with a person can be a vital first step in the healing and may be treated by a therapist at a later time. All of this is as important for serving someone experiencing secondary trauma as it is with someone experiencing primary trauma.

Secondary Trauma at the Disaster Scene

Many disasters involve responders from a wide variety of disciplines. Serving near us may be behavioral health responders, medical health responders, case workers and other Disaster Spiritual Care responders. Perhaps there will also be governmental emergency managers, fire and police responders, communication specialists, and many others—each with specific and unique responsibilities. At some point, there could be volunteers coming to the area from other communities to clear trees, mitigate mold, bring needed supplies, repair homes, and so on.

No matter their response mode or even their length of service as a responder, these are all people. Often they work tirelessly and well past fatigue in order to serve others. This is true for us, and it is true for all others: All responders are vulnerable to secondary trauma. Every responder in a disaster zone is likely to see, hear, feel, smell, and even taste things that are far outside normal human living. This means all of us are vulnerable to secondary trauma.

When deployed to a disaster, our focus is naturally upon those who directly experienced whatever kind of disaster happened. But, as Disaster Spiritual Care workers, we need also to be aware that traumatized persons may be among those who serve alongside us.

In 2005, while in Ocean Springs, Mississippi, following Hurricane Katrina, I served alongside responders of all types. A large group of Red Cross volunteers was staying and working at the same location I was. Among them were some behavioral health team members. I watched their tireless work at helping people who had been hammered by that vicious storm. One evening when another hectic day had finally settled down, a number of us, including those Red Cross team members, were "decompressing" after supper. Suddenly one of the Red Cross Behavioral Health Team members— a psychologist in her regular life—broke into tears. "I don't know if

I'm helping anybody. They need so much!" She sobbed and sobbed. She was not weak. Her work in those days clearly displayed her strength and training. She was a strong person experiencing secondary trauma. In addition to her trauma, she was now also experiencing shame at "losing it" in front of others.

I was at that center as a helper. I didn't yet know anything about Disaster Spiritual Care. With others, I tried to offer support, but in retrospect, we all completely missed the mark. She needed more than nice words. She needed focused attention from a trained responder. The next day, she did her work quite well. But during quiet times, we could see in her eyes the painful struggle she was in. We had failed her.

There is no recipe for helping other responders who may be experiencing secondary trauma. Disaster responders tend to be a special lot. We thrive on the energy and sense of purpose we bring to a disaster scene. Disaster responders—perhaps a bit more than others—hate the idea of being perceived by others as weak. We will give ourselves the TS card and cover our reactions, holding tightly within ourselves any trauma responses we have. Responders are not typically show-offs who are trying to impress others with how much we can handle but professionals who understand that our strength can offer strength to

SOME COMMON SIGNS OF TRAUMA

- Irritability
- Inappropriate anger
- Oppositional behavior
- Intrusive thoughts and memories
- Withdrawal
- Avoidance
- Anxiety
- Panic
- Hypervigilance
- Physical symptoms including rapid pulse, headaches, gastrointestinal problems
- Rapid mood swings
- Changes in appetite or sleep patterns

others. This "countenance" is important. But it can also be a big problem.

Our purpose is not to deceive others with "pretend" strength, which is dishonest and can do more harm than good. Self-care, which we all know to be important (whether we practice it or not), must always be girded by self-awareness. Perhaps our primary failing with the Red Cross psychologist was that we didn't urge her to take a bit of time off—or, at the very least, to put that idea into her mind.

Some things just don't hide well. The "thousand-yard stare," the wide eyes, difficulty with concentration, withdrawal, uncontrolled emotions—these are just a few signs that a responder is in trouble. These are some key things we should watch for in other responders and be aware of in ourselves.

There are direct things we can do to help another responder, particularly if we know that person. We can simply observe that we are concerned about him or her. We may get a denial, but the conversation is opened, and he or she may come back at a later time.

We can even be more direct. "I've noticed you staring off into space a lot lately. Are you okay?"

We have a judgment to make. Our gut reactions can inform us if the direct approach will be useful or may push that person more deeply into denial. The best we can do is trust our instincts.

Our instincts may, on the other hand, tell us if it is best to ask to speak to that person's supervisor. This will probably feel awkward, as if we are "telling on" someone. But it is worth it if we save that one from even deeper difficulties. If that person seems to be impaired, it will be important for the supervisor to know. The supervisor needs to know this not only for the responder's well-being but also for the well-being of the disaster survivors he or she serves.

But the big thing is this: don't do nothing. We need to check our own level of denial about that person's possible struggles. There are many stories about responders who "burn out" after years of responding and may self-medicate or engage in other kinds of dangerous behavior. This is hard and a sensitive issue. But this is always important.

Summary

Secondary trauma is something experienced by many, including those who have earlier unresolved traumas, those who serve others, and possibly even ourselves. Understanding it may help us better assist others and may very well make our own responses more effective and less damaging. It should not be ignored.

Preview

We become hypothetical in Chapter Ten. Following our consideration of secondary trauma in others and in ourselves, we will now turn our attention to the possibility that it can also be experienced by large parts of a population. If so, is there a role that Disaster Spiritual Care can play to help heal a whole society?

10

The 9/11 Sky

<u>Secondary Trauma And a Big "What if"</u>

But what if you're wrong
What if there's more
What if there's hope
You never dreamed of hoping for
What if you jump?
Just close your eyes
What if the arms that catch you
Catch you by surprise?
What if He's more than enough?
What if it's love?

"What If," Lyrics by Nichole Nordeman, released by
Prince in 2015

The morning of September 11, 2001, was absolutely beautiful in eastern Pennsylvania, where I live. I was at my desk in the church at which I served preparing the agenda for our regular Tuesday morning staff meeting when the phone rang. It was my wife, Lois. "Have you seen what's going on?" Her voice was urgent. "Something's going on at the World Trade Center in New York. A plane hit it!"

I quickly found a TV, turned it on, and saw the North Tower with horrible smoke coming from an upper floor. The rest is history.

But, throughout the TV coverage of this attack, broadcasters referred to the beauty of the sky that day and how it stood in such stark contrast to what was going on before our eyes. The cameras easily captured the contrast.

I don't know how many times in the years since, when I have noticed beautiful bright blue skies with puffy clouds, I have powerfully recalled the vision of that day and felt the emotion of it. That happened a decade and a half ago, but a 9/11 sky will still do that to me. So many things have changed in my life since then, but a 9/11 sky will take me back to September 11, 2001, as if it were all happening right then.

I was 100 miles away.

Sometimes someone will mention the assassination of President Kennedy. For the briefest moment I am climbing the crowded steps in the main stairway at my high school in 1963 and hearing someone shout, "President Kennedy's been shot!" I could take you to the very step I was on when I heard that shout. I wish I still had the long journal entry I wrote later that night in which I expressed my certainty that the president was not dead but that all of this was a cover for his being off on some secret mission to the Soviet Union to talk peace. I can still see that denial-filled paper on the desk before me.

Something gets mentioned about the assassination of Martin Luther King, Jr. and I am suddenly in my old white Ford Pinto, pulling into the parking area of my college fraternity house, hearing a radio bulletin about his death, and racing inside to join the large group crowded around the TV.

These events of my earlier life were traumatic for me. Even today, a beautiful sky, a certain set of steps in a stairwell, or pulling into a certain parking space will bring back those feelings. It is far more than just being reminded of them. Reminders happen in my cognitive brain. But I am re-experiencing these, not remembering them. My amygdala is sending messages to my body, warning me of a threat, and I am back there again—if only for that brief moment.

I was not the only one, of course, who experiences these things. Over the years, I've had conversations with others who clearly and in great detail "remember" these same events. We'll express some "wow" comments with each other, and then we'll move on.

Or do we?

What if more than a single person can be affected by secondary trauma? What if, in fact, a whole segment of the population can be affected by it? What if this segment can be traumatized by watching a disaster unfold in real time through the media? What if we could better understand how widespread secondary trauma actually affects people? What if we could more clearly identify behaviors that might point to widespread trauma? What if secondary traumas pile up inside people if they are not processed? What if trained Disaster Spiritual Care responders attended to this kind of trauma as part of their calling?

That is a lot of "what ifs." We conclude this book with a rather big "What if?" What if secondary trauma is widespread? What might we expect to observe and how might we respond to it?

In the science of logic there is something known as the "material conditional." It is a simple idea on the surface and is familiar to us all. It simply means, "If *this* is true, then *that* is also true." An example can be found in a teacher's instructing her class: "If you participate in class (condition A), then you will get extra points (condition B)." The simplicity of this statement is simply that if A is true, then B is also true.

If major segments of a population share a secondary trauma, *then* what? What is the "then?" Is there a truth that follows that makes this into a material conditional—a natural consequence truth? Depending on how we answer that question, the whole scope of Disaster Spiritual Care might be redefined. That is a big statement, and I am aware of no definitive studies that have been published that can assist us in anticipating the "then" part of the condition.

So, what I am about to share is highly intuitive and not yet based on scientific study. My purpose is to share some ideas and invite readers to explore any useful paths we might discover. Everything in this section requires more study. But important ideas always begin with unproven notions. The notion I put before us all is this: "*If* major segments of our population share a secondary trauma, *then* the work of Disaster Spiritual Care responders cannot be restricted to specific disasters."

The Role of Terror

To explore this, let us focus primarily on assumed secondary trauma derived from worldwide and domestic acts of terror. The National Counterterrorism Center (https://www.nctc.gov) identified 545 acts of terror or important terror-related events in the world between 1975 and 2015. If we chart these on a simple line graph, as I have in Figure 1, it is easy to see that the frequency of terroristic acts is generally on the rise. *Please notice that I have not included the x-axis numbers on this or the following graphs.* On this and each of the graphs that follow, I have included numbers or percentages at certain peaks and valleys to help understand the scale that is represented. What we are interested in here is comparing line *shapes* rather than specific numbers.

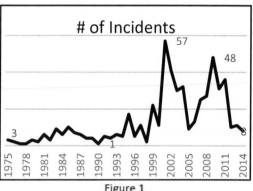

Figure 1

What we will also notice is that the graph of terror incidents is not a straight line. There are years when terrorist acts are far more frequent than others. But raw numbers do not necessarily reflect how horrific the events were in any one year. The simple lower number of events in a year do not necessarily describe the impact of terror. Some events are far more horrific than others and can be assumed to have far more impact. Likewise, some world events impact Americans far more than others. This is our first piece of data.

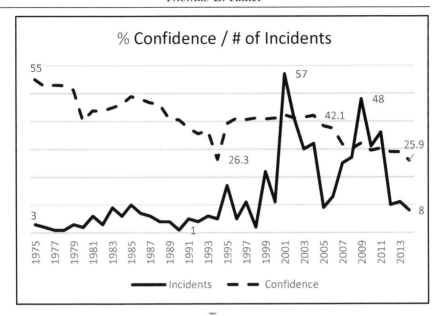

Figure 2

Next, we think of American institutions and the confidence levels that Americans have placed in them over these forty years. The Gallup Organization has included surveys of confidence in major institutions since 1975 (http://www.gallup.com/poll/1597/Confidence-Institutions.aspx). Notice in the dashed line that the public's rating of "A Great Deal or Quite a Lot" of confidence in American institutions is on the decline. In this graph, confidence findings for a number of American institutions was traced. This traces a historical average of survey results of the public's confidence in six American institutions: the institutional church, the US Supreme Court, the banking system, public schools, newspapers, and the US Congress. These six represent key segments of our complex culture, though certainly not all of it. Confidence in these American institutions has declined from a combined average of 55.5 percent in 1975 to 25.9 percent in 2014. This is a very significant decrease.

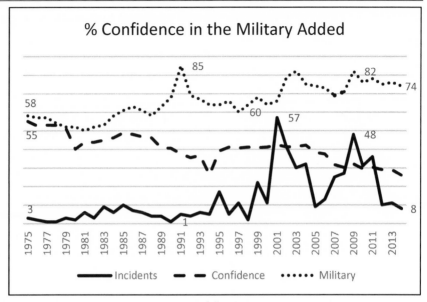

Figure 3

Finally, let us add a third line—confidence in the US Military. The dotted line reflects Gallup's findings for confidence in the military as a part of the same series of surveys noted above. The importance of this line will become clearer shortly. But notice in the dotted line that it shows far greater confidence in the military than it does in the other American institutions. Notice also that, while the line shifts from time to time, the public's rating of "A Great Deal or Quite a Lot" of confidence in the military has actually increased as confidence in other institutions has decreased. For reference, those with complete or a lot of confidence in the military has risen from 58 percent to 74 percent of respondents. This is a rather substantial increase.

Terrorism was certainly not the only factor that might have caused generalized trauma or secondary trauma in the US public throughout these forty years. We so clearly remember 9/11, but many other events have pierced our hearts as well. As terrorist attacks became more frequent, we also saw the Iranian Hostage Crisis begin in 1978. John Lennon was shot to death in 1980. The AIDS Epidemic hit the U.S. in 1981. The Challenger Space Shuttle shook us in 1986. The anthrax scare took root on the heels of 9/11 in 2001. We witnessed the DC sniper shootings of 2002. The Asian Tsunami of 2004 killed

230,000 people in fourteen countries. The Great Recession took root in 2008. A number of disastrous earthquakes struck during these decades, including the great 2010 earthquake in Haiti, and we experienced several episodes of clustered tornados in the United States. A series of school and theater shootings took place, including the Sandy Hook Elementary School shooting in 2012. Many other domestic and international disasters (both natural and man-made) consumed our attention during these decades. It was a time filled with traumas. But, as traumatic as any of these things have been, none have impacted Americans for a longer period of time than terrorism. Also, 24/7 cable TV news rose to dominate the broadcast market and social media burst onto the scene, Americans gained access to round-the-clock intimate coverage of terrorist events—a far greater exposure than in earlier years.

The rise in cable TV news has been matched—and eclipsed—by the number of persons (young and old) who follow disasters on social media. A 2013 study by researchers at the University of California-Irvine surveyed a national sample of 4,675 adults two to four weeks after the Boston Marathon bombings to assess acute stress responses to the bombings. Their findings indicated that people exposed to six or more hours per day of bombing-related media coverage were nine times more likely to report high acute stress than those with minimal media exposure (less than one hour daily).

E. Alison Holman, associate professor of nursing science at UC Irvine and the study's lead author, noted:

> We were very surprised that repeated media exposure was so strongly associated with acute stress symptoms. We suspect that there's something about repeated exposure to violent images or sounds that keeps traumatic events alive and can prolong the stress response in vulnerable people. There is mounting evidence that live and video images of traumatic events can trigger flashbacks and encourage fear conditioning. If repeatedly viewing

traumatic images reactivates fear or threat responses in the brain and promotes rumination, there could be serious health consequences...When you repeatedly see images of a person with gruesome injuries after an event is over, it's like the event continues and has its own presence in your life. Prolonged media exposure can turn what was an acute experience into a chronic form of stress. People may not realize how stressful these media-based exposures are. Looking at these images over and over again is not productive and may be harmful (Ricco, 2013).

In a 2015 study done by The University of Bradford in England, researcher Pam Ramsden found that more than a fifth of respondents scored high on clinical measures of PTSD from seeing pictures on social media—even though they hadn't experienced the traumatic events first-hand (Naubert, 2013).

What if the rise of access to coverage of terrorism and other traumatic events and the decline in public confidence in major institutions are somehow related? Let's look for clues in an unlikely place—our youngest children.

The Task of Attachment

Infants and toddlers are terrific at letting caregivers know that they need something—food, diaper change, cuddling, etc. Even non-parents certainly have surely observed this fascinating skill in other people's children. Young children just know how to keep caregivers attached, available, and responsive.

John Bowlby, a British psychologist and psychiatrist, helped the world understand why. He was later joined by Mary Ainsworth in the development of what is termed Attachment Theory. This unique skill has both developmental and evolutionary roots. Young children know how to keep their primary caregiver near in order to survive and thrive. Mary Ainsworth developed the Strange Situation procedure in 1969 to observe attachment relationships between a caregiver and a child. In this procedure, young children aged nine to eighteen months were brought into a room by their mothers. Upon a certain signal, the mothers would leave. Then later they would return.

Most of these children experienced some degree of distress when their mothers left. Some, after only a brief time, began to lose control of themselves in a variety of ways, including crying, tantrums, withdrawal, or other "signal-sending" behaviors. Their anxiety at the separation grew worse and worse as time passed. When the mothers were brought back into the room, rather interesting things happened. About 60 percent of the children responded happily and affectionately to the reunion. They were labeled "securely attached" children. But another 20 percent reacted quite differently. They showed some relief at the reunion but then displayed sometimes quite high levels of anger at the mother as well. These were labeled "ambivalent attached" children. Yet another 20 percent of children hardly noticed the mother's leaving or her return. These were labeled "avoidant attached" children.

Still other experiments with young children, developed by Dr. Edward Tronick more than a quarter century ago, disclosed another key response of young children. His Still Face Experiment featured mothers who, upon a signal, became completely unresponsive to their child. Videos of these experiments (watch at www.youtube.com, search "Still Face Experiment") showed how quickly these children became completely disorganized emotionally and physically. They waved their arms then lost all control of their limbs. They began to slobber, cried and wailed, and did anything and everything to get their mom, their caretaker, to reconnect with them. They displayed enormous anxiety.

Bowlby maintained that such reactions of young children are an evolutionary product designed over the millennia to help humanity survive. He also maintained that these attachment styles and needs don't go away but remain throughout life. And that's where Bowlby and Ainsworth's work connects to our "what if."

Terrorism and other traumatic events touch deep survival needs within us. Anxiety grows with the intensity, proximity, and "layering on" of these experiences. Sinclair and LoCicero observe that, "under immediate threat beyond one's personal ability to manage, it would be adaptive to seek protection from a stronger, tougher resource, either from the entire group or from a designated leader" (Sinclair & LoCicero, 2010).

Thus, we can see that, following 9/11, for example, confidence in institutions (Figure 2) spikes. We lay our inbred survival instincts at the feet of our leaders and our institutions. It is the "attention seeking" and "survival seeking" response of the young children model applied to adulthood concerns. Simply put, we want our leaders to help us survive.

But, unlike a mother who can mitigate a child's anxiety by simply coming back into the room, leaders and institutions cannot instantly make us feel safe. When the threat or perception of a threat continues, we may find leaders as unresponsive as the unresponsive mothers. Anger rises. For the 40 percent with less than secure attachment profiles, there may come the onset of behaviors that echo the disorganization of the young children in that experiment. Seeking different leadership, attacking present leadership, mistrusting institutions, ignoring cultural norms, going public with previously hidden angers toward people or groups of people perceived as somehow threatening—any of these things (and certainly many more) would be expected.

Doesn't that describe, for instance, the political campaign of 2016? Truth was not as important as attachment. Civility was not as important as power and promises of protection. Values were not as important as attention-seeking. Norms were discarded, and a yearning for "dream-like" former times of safety and security dominated. In the wake of the election with its surprising results, political pundits referred again and again to hidden anger in the American electorate—an anger that was commonly characterized as stemming from being ignored. Was this anger at being ignored?

Perhaps. Or perhaps it was anger stemming from feeling very vulnerable.

Each terrorist attack needed to be associated with one, some leader's failure and two, someone else's promise that there was a way to make it all go away. The rise of ISIS became the ever-present tinnitus in the ears of the traumatized. And this was indistinguishable from the tinnitus of economic uncertainty and, for many whites, the loss of presumed social rank and privilege. We wanted a strong parental figure to come back into the room and protect us.

Our accumulated trauma and fear had reduced us, I believe, to a culture of nine to eighteen month old's survival instincts, complete with the undergirding of ambivalent, avoidant, and angry attachment issues and behaviors.

An Issue for Disaster Spiritual Caregivers?

If, at the scene of a disaster, we observed an individual displaying anger, disorganized behaviors, yearning for a pre-disaster time, disregard for others and/or withdrawal, we would surely see this person as someone to whom we would like to offer our care.

What if we could develop a Disaster Spiritual Care model that could attend to the needs of a broader public? I have come to believe that this is both necessary and extremely challenging. And I certainly do not have the recipe for such a model to share.

But what if we pondered it? What if we gave good and prayerful consideration to the needs of those traumatized by the events of the past forty years, and especially the past twenty? What if we found ways to look past the behaviors and saw distressed others as ones whom God also loves and has sent us to serve? What if we found ways to push through the wall so well described in "Please Hear What I'm Not Saying"? What if we designed service that is consistent with our beliefs that God cares about this creation and the beloved community of people that inhabit it? What if we expanded Disaster Spiritual Care to include the entire culture?

Here are some initial suggestions of where we might begin.

- Sometimes, if I am planning something but hit a wall, I will lay a reminder of it on a table that I regularly walk past. These repeated glances have frequently turned a light on for me, and what was hidden becomes quite clear. Lay this concern about how we can attend to corporate secondary trauma on a mental table. Each time you "pass" it, glance at the idea and see if you notice anything new.

- Become even better educated about trauma and secondary trauma with special attention to common symptoms.

- Talk about your ideas with others—both responders and non-responders. Frequently, we best discover what we are thinking when we hear ourselves talk about it. Especially reflect on the idea of how we have become a dismissive society—dismissive of cultural norms, dismissive of the needs and dreams of people unlike us, dismissive of language and behaviors that not long ago would have been quite offensive. Why do so many dismiss so much?

- Join the Disaster Spiritual Care community site at sacredturf.org. Find the "Community" tab, click on "Keep the Book Open", and share your ideas with others. Your kernel of an idea may spark a whole new one in someone else.

- Observe the culture around you. When additional shared traumas occur, what do you notice in the way people initially react? How do reactions change over time? As people speak about the present event, do they also mention earlier ones? Compare your observations with others and share them at sacredturf.org.

Together, maybe we can invent a model that Disaster Spiritual Care responders can use to help whole communities of people.

Summary

Trauma can be experienced indirectly when someone is exposed to the disasters of others. It may be of significance that American culture displays symptoms often understood as signs of trauma. Is there a role for Disaster Spiritual Care to a larger society?

Afterword

As noted earlier, Disaster Spiritual Care is only now reaching maturity as a disaster response mode. Its value for those whose lives have been affected by disaster is increasingly being recognized both, within the field and within the wider public. I thank you for your interest, and I encourage you to participate in its continued development and growth.

Some worry that spiritual care does not belong within the broad range of government-related response because of appropriate concerns for the separation of government and religion. It is my hope that one benefit of this book will be to more clearly illustrate that spiritual care does not proselytize, preach, or recruit. It is focused on the deep needs of those who have just come through what may be the worst season of their lives and seeks to assist them with re-discovering the hope for the future that empowers them to recover.

If you are new to Disaster Spiritual Care, I hope that this book has provided some new insights into its purposes and services. I would encourage you to continue your study of Disaster Spiritual Care. Many faith-based organizations offer training and credentials for those interested in becoming responders. The American Red Cross has encouraged its many chapters to offer this kind of care to those they serve. Some states are now developing state-wide response organizations. Other states, I believe, will soon join them.

If you wish, you can follow my blog at sacredturf.org. There I regularly expand on subjects introduced here. From time to time, guest bloggers will enrich your experience with their own views. It is also a good place to ask the Disaster Spiritual Care community the questions you may have. In this sense, I encourage you to keep the book of hope open for those you may serve, as well as to keep the book of growth open for yourself.

Peace,

Tom Kadel

Appendix A
8 Things You Should Know About Disaster Spiritual Care

1) It is about hope

Disaster Spiritual Care helps those affected by disaster to draw upon their own emotional and spiritual resources to find the hope necessary for recovery

WISDOM (1): *"Hope is the foundation of resiliency."*

2) It is about spiritual care

Disaster Spiritual Care provides care to all persons regardless of religion. When possible and welcomed, the caregiver will facilitate contact with one's religious community or tradition.

WISDOM (1): *"All persons have a spiritual core, even if it is not a part of a religious system."*

WISDOM (2): *"A national poll sponsored by the Red Cross after 9/11 reported that 60 percent of respondents said they would be more likely to seek help from a spiritual caregiver than either a physician (45%) or a mental health professional (40%)."* Harold G. Koenig, *In the Wake of Disaster: Religious Responses to Terrorism and Catastrophe.* Templeton Press, 2008

3) It does not proselytize

Spiritual Care providers recognize that survivors of disaster are often extremely vulnerable and will not abuse this imbalance of power to serve any ends except the survivors' well-being.

WISDOM: *"It is all about recovery, not recruitment."*

4) It is effective throughout disaster's life-cycle.

Survivors often go through "why" questions to "how" questions.
- "Why did this happen?"
- "How do I go on?"

Throughout, these questions have practical and deeply spiritual levels. Spiritual care belongs to the entire life-cycle.

WISDOM: *"Every disaster has a life-cycle, and so do its survivors."*

5) It is team-oriented

Spiritual care works cooperatively with other responders—especially behavioral health providers and local faith-based leaders. Spiritual care providers are trained to detect underlying psychological and emotional conditions in order to make referrals to specialists in those areas. They also recognize that each faith tradition has intricacies that they may not be qualified to interpret. Those intricacies are best addressed by representatives from the survivor's own faith tradition.

WISDOM: *"No one is everyone. Anything is too often nothing."*

6) It recognizes the power of stories

Stories can not only knit people together but also re-knit hope and resiliency within the individual. Spiritual stories (even when not framed in spiritual language) have the power to give shape to individual stories and allow the spiritual provider to accompany survivors on what may very well be the most difficult journey of their lives.

WISDOM: *"The most powerful accompaniment is being with others through their stories."*

7) It is about presence

The most powerful tool the spiritual care provider has is the power of presence. Words are frequently far less important that the provider's presence with the survivor.

WISDOM (1): *"Presence commonly trumps words."*

WISDOM (2): *"If you cannot improve upon silence, don't try."*

8) It is about being well-trained and committed to common principles

Wanting to help those in distress is common human nature. But, as in other response disciplines, harm can result from untrained response or compromised principles.

WISDOM (1): *"Always know how to 'do no harm.'"*

WISDOM (2) *"Wanting to help is eclipsed by knowing how and why."*

OVERALL WISDOM (1): *"God/The Deity (however understood) always precedes responders to the site of a disaster and is always present after those responders have departed."*

OVERALL WISDOM (2): *"Spiritual Care providers are the hands, arms, feet, and speech of God/The Deity, not of themselves."*

Appendix B
National Voluntary Organizations Active in Disaster Points of Consensus

Ratified by Full Membership, 2009

DISASTER SPIRITUAL CARE

In 2006, the National Voluntary Organizations Active in Disaster's Emotional and Spiritual Care Committee published <u>Light Our Way</u> to inform, encourage, and affirm those who respond to disasters and to encourage standards insuring those affected by disaster receive appropriate and respectful spiritual care services. As a natural next step following the publication of <u>Light Our Way</u>, and in the spirit of the NVOAD "Four C's" (cooperation, communication, coordination, and collaboration), the Emotional and Spiritual Care Committee then began working to define more specific standards for disaster spiritual care providers. The following ten "points of consensus" set a foundation for that continuing work.

1.   Basic concepts of disaster spiritual care[1]

Spirituality is an essential part of humanity. Disaster significantly disrupts people's spiritual lives. Nurturing people's spiritual needs contributes to holistic healing. Every person can benefit from spiritual care in time of disaster.

2.   Types of disaster spiritual care[2]

Spiritual care in disaster includes many kinds of caring gestures. Spiritual care providers are from diverse backgrounds. Adherence to common standards and principles in spiritual care ensures that this service is delivered and received appropriately.

3. Local community resources

As an integral part of the pre-disaster community, local spiritual care providers and communities of faith are primary resources for post-disaster spiritual care. Because local communities of faith are uniquely equipped to provide healing care, any spiritual care services entering from outside of the community support but do not substitute for local efforts. The principles of the National VOAD — cooperation, coordination, communication and collaboration — are essential to the delivery of disaster spiritual care.

4. Disaster emotional care and its relationship to disaster spiritual care[3]

Spiritual care providers partner with mental health professionals in caring for communities in disaster. Spiritual and emotional care share some similarities but are distinct healing modalities. Spiritual care providers can be an important asset in referring individuals to receive care for their mental health and vice versa.

5. Disaster spiritual care in response and recovery[4]

Spiritual care has an important role in all phases of a disaster, including short-term response through long-term recovery. Assessing and providing for the spiritual needs of individuals, families, and communities can kindle important capacities of hope and resilience. Specific strategies for spiritual care during the various phases can bolster these strengths.

6. Disaster emotional and spiritual care for the caregiver

Providing spiritual care in disaster can be an overwhelming experience. The burdens of caring for others in this context can lead to compassion fatigue. Understanding important strategies for self-care is essential for spiritual care providers. Disaster response agencies have a responsibility to model healthy work and life habits to care for their own staff in time of disaster.[5] Post-care processes for spiritual and emotional care providers are essential.

7.   Planning, preparedness, training, and mitigation as spiritual care components[6]

Faith community leaders have an important role in planning and mitigation efforts. By preparing their congregations and themselves for disaster, they contribute toward building resilient communities. Training for the role of disaster spiritual care provider is essential before disaster strikes.

8.   Disaster spiritual care in diversity

Respect is foundational to disaster spiritual care. Spiritual care providers demonstrate respect for diverse cultural and religious values by recognizing the right of each faith group and individual to hold to their existing values and traditions. Spiritual care providers:

- refrain from manipulation, disrespect, or exploitation of those impacted by disaster and trauma.
- respect the freedom from unwanted gifts of religious literature or symbols, evangelistic and sermonizing speech, and/or forced acceptance of specific moral values and traditions.[7]
- respect diversity and differences, including but not limited to culture, gender, age, sexual orientation, spiritual/religious practices, and disability.

9.   Disaster, trauma and vulnerability

People impacted by disaster and trauma are vulnerable. There is an imbalance of power between disaster responders and those receiving care. To avoid exploiting that imbalance, spiritual care providers refrain from using their position, influence, knowledge, or professional affiliation for unfair advantage or for personal, organizational, or agency gain.

Disaster response will not be used to further a particular political or religious perspective or cause—responses will be carried out according to the need of individuals, families, and communities. The promise, delivery, or distribution of assistance will not be tied to the embracing or acceptance of a particular political or religious creed. [8]

10.   Ethics and Standards of Care

NVOAD members affirm the importance of cooperative standards of care and agreed ethics. Adherence to common standards and principles in spiritual care ensures that this service is delivered and received appropriately. Minimally, any guidelines developed for spiritual care in times of disaster should clearly articulate the above consensus points in addition to the following:

- Standards for personal and professional integrity
- Accountability structures regarding the behavior of individuals and groups
- Concern for honoring confidentiality*
- Description of professional boundaries that guarantee safety of clients*, including standards regarding interaction with children, youth, and vulnerable adults
- Policies regarding criminal background checks for service providers
- Mechanisms for ensuring that caregivers function at levels appropriate to their training and educational backgrounds*
- Strong adherence to standards rejecting violence against particular groups
- Policies when encountering persons needing referral to other agencies or services
- Guidelines regarding financial remuneration for services provided

Works Cited

Altmaier, Elizabeth. "About Reconstructing Meaning after Trauma." *Elizabeth Altmaier, PhD*. Web.

Baken, David. *The Duality of Human Existence*. Boston: Beacon, 1966. Print.

Bonanno, George. "Loss, Trauma and Human Resilience." *The American Psychologist* (2004): 21. Web.

Buechner, Frederick. *Now and Then*. New York: Harper and Row, 1983. Print.

Cheever, John. "Montraldo." *New Yorker*. 6 June 1964: Print.

"Confidence in Institutions." *Poll*. Gallup Organization, Web.

"Counterrorism Guide." *The National Counterterrorism Center*. The National Counterterrorism Center. Web.

Crites, Stephen. "The Narrative Quality of Experience." *Journal of the American Academy of Religion* 39.3 (1971). Web.

"Critical Incident Stress Management." CISM International, Web.

Crone, Travis S., and Denise R. Beike. "1. Priming the Nonconscious Goal to Self-Actualize: Can Even the Highest Order Goals Be Primed Nonconsciously?" *The Humanistic Psychologist* 40.3 (2012). Web.

Dyson, Michael Eric. *Come Hell or High Water: Hurricane Katrina and the Color of Disaster*. New York: Basic Civitas, 2005. Print.

"Erikson's Psychosocial Stages Summary Chart." *VeryWell*. Web.

Ferguson, David. "Orlando Survivor Patience Carter Describes Horrific Scene: 'The Guilt of Being Alive Is Heavy'." *RawStory*. 14 June 2016.

Figley, C.R., ed. *Compassion Fatigue: Secondary Traumatic Stress Disorders from Treating the Traumatized*. New York: Brunner/Mazel, 1995. Print.

Finn, Charles. "Please Hear What I'm Not Saying." Web. Used with permission.

Frankl, Viktor. *Man's Search for Meaning*. Boston: Beacon, 1992. Print.

Gonsales, Laurence. *Surviving Survival: The Art and Science of Resilience*. New York: W.W. Horton, 2012. Print.

Goodstein, Laurie. "Poll Shows Major Shift in Identity of U.S. Jews." *New York Times*. 1 Oct. 2013. Web.

Herman, Judith. *Trauma and Recovery: The Aftermath of Violence – from Domestic Abuse to Political Terror*. New York: Basic, 1992. Print.

"Importance-of-religion-in-ones-life." *Pew Forum*. 2016. Web.

Janoff-Bulman, Ronnie. *Shattered Assumptions*. New York: Free, 1992. Print. Towards a New Psychology of Trauma

Lipka, Michael. "Why America's 'nones' Left Religion behind." *Pew Research*. 24 Aug. 2016. Web.

Malamud, Bernard. *God's Grace*. New York: Farrar Straus Giroux, 1982. Print.

McAdams, Dan P., and Brady K. Jones. *Making Meaning in the Wake of Trauma: Resilience and Redemption*. For E. M. Altmaier (Ed.), *Reconstructing Meaning after Trauma* (forthcoming 2016).

McAdams, Dan P. "The Psychology of Life Stories." *Review of General Psychology* 5.2 (2001): 100-22. Web.

McAdams, Dan P. "Coding Autobiographical Episodes for Themes of Agency and Communion." *Sesp.northwestern.edu*. Northwestern University, 2001 (r). Web.

Morgan, Alice. "What Is Narrative Therapy?" *The Dulwich Centre*. Web.

Morris, Michael. "Muslims Fastest Growing." *CNS News*. Web.

Mother Teresa. *Mother Teresa: Come Be My Light*. Ed. Brian Kolodiejchuk. New York: Doubleday, 2016. Print.

Massey, Kevin. National Voluntary Organizations Active in Disaster. *Light Our Way*. 2013. A Guide for Spiritual Care in Times of Disaster.

Naubert, Rick. "Prolonged Viewing of Boston Marathon Bombings Media Coverage Tied to Acute Stress." PsychCentral. 2013.

Web.

Red Rubber Ball. By Paul Simon and Bruce Woodley. Perf. The Cyrcle. 1966. Web. Georgy Girl Album

Ricco, Laura. "Prolonged Viewing of Boston Marathon Bombings Media Coverage Tied to Acute Stress." School of Social Ecology, 2013. University of California – Irvine. Web.

Sinclair, Samuel J., and Alice Locicero. "Do Fears of Terrorism Predict Trust in Government?" *Journal of Aggression, Conflict and Peace Research* 2.1 (2010). Web.

Thompson, Jeff. "Is Nonverbal Communication a Numbers Game?" *Psychology Today*. Psychology Today, 2011. Web.

"Trauma." *Amerian Psychological Association*. Web. 14 July 2016.

Walsh, Froma. "Traumatic Loss and Major Disasters: Strengthening Family and Community Resilience." *Family Process* 46.2 (2007). Web.

Wilder, Thornton. *The Bridge of San Luis Rey*. New York: Perennial Classics, 2003. Print.

Index

About the Author

THOMAS E. KADEL is a member of the clergy of the Evangelical Lutheran Church in America and serves as co-director of the Pennsylvania Disaster Spiritual Care Network. He is a Spiritual Care Team member and instructor for the American Red Cross, Supervisor of the Spiritual Partners service of Lutheran Disaster Response of Eastern Pennsylvania, and a responder and instructor for the Keystone Crisis Intervention Team. He also serves as an advocate for the poor in seventeen nations in the Caribbean and Latin America through Food for the Poor. He lives in Harleysville, Pennsylvania, with his wife Lois.